294.34435
Mulligan, Beth Ann.
The Dharma of modern
mindfulness : discovering the
Buddhist teachings at the heart
of mindfulness-based stress
reduction c2017

Discard
Santa Maria Library

"Written with disarming ca_____
reader on an intimate journ_____
reduction (MBSR), the go_____
The author seamlessly reve_____
MBSR and core teachings from Buddhist psy_____ _____ underlie the program. If you want to understand n_____
more deeply than ever, this wise and genero_____
be missed!"

  —Christopher Germer, PhD, author of _The___
  Path to Self-Compassion ___ditor of *Mindfulness and*
  Psychotherapy, and le___
  Medical School

Funded by a California
State Library, Crisis
Collections grant 17/18

"An invaluable companion for anyone taking a mindfulness-based stress reduction course. It makes the teachings of MBSR come alive in a deep, meaningful, and easy-to-understand way. Highly recommended!"

  —Kristin Neff, PhD, associate professor in the
  department of educational psychology at The University
  of Texas at Austin, and author of *Self-Compassion*

"As a medical professional, Zen practitioner, and teacher of mindfulness-based stress reduction (MBSR), Beth Ann Mulligan is able to weave together different perspectives to illuminate a path toward greater health, happiness, and freedom. This book has the power to transform our individual and collective lives."

  —Shauna Shapiro, PhD, professor at Santa Clara
  University, author, speaker, and mindfulness consultant

"What a gem of a book! Beth Ann Mulligan leads us, with her many years of experience in teaching mindfulness-based stress reduction (MBSR) and even more years of being a dedicated Dharma student, intimately through one eight-week MBSR course, chock-full of wonderful people, stories, and insights. She weaves into this the Dharma teachings as they show up in the classroom, without ever being mentioned in there. She makes the invisible visible and understandable for us, so we can teach MBSR and other mindfulness-based classes from a place of deeper understanding. This is a must-read for all MBSR and mindfulness-based intervention teachers, and anybody else curious about how the Buddhist teachings are informing modern mindfulness."

—**Christiane Wolf, MD, PhD**, certified MBSR teacher, adjunct faculty of the Center for Mindfulness at the University of Massachusetts Medical School, director of MBSR programs and senior teacher at InsightLA, vipassana and mindful self-compassion (MSC) teacher, and coauthor of A *Clinician's Guide to Teaching Mindfulness*

"A wise and openhearted invitation to the teachings of modern mindfulness and Buddhism. Beth Ann Mulligan tells stories and offers the teachings that arise directly from our human experience, showing how the path of modern mindfulness parallels the ancient teachings of Buddhism. Weaving these two streams, Beth offers us a way of finding freedom right in the middle of the challenge of our lives. Down-to-earth and inclusive, this book is a wonderful introduction to mindfulness-based stress reduction and the basic teachings of Buddhism."

—**Roshi David Dae An Rynick**, author of *This Truth Never Fails*

"Beth Ann Mulligan's wise, clear, and compassionate writing brings the ancient teachings of the Buddha to life as she describes her lived experience of teaching mindfulness-based stress reduction. The authenticity, integrity, and vulnerability that she shares in her stories and teachings offer us an intimacy with what it means to be fully human. This beautiful book has touched my heart deeply and enriched my understanding of the roots of mindfulness-based programs. It is a true gift, a shining pearl in the growing field of modern mindfulness."

—**Diane Reibel, PhD**, director of the Mindfulness Institute at Thomas Jefferson University Hospital, coauthor of *Teaching Mindfulness*, and coeditor of *Resources for Teaching Mindfulness*

"This beautifully structured, wise, and compassionate book takes us behind the scenes of a mindfulness-based stress reduction (MBSR) class for an insider's view. Beth then offers in-depth teachings from the Buddhist tradition that underlie MBSR. Most importantly, Beth's years of personal meditation practice and teaching shine through; the writing is infused with both theory and a deep experiential knowing. It is sure to be a seminal work for students and teachers of mindfulness alike."

—**Diana Winston**, director of mindfulness education at UCLA's Mindful Awareness Research Center, and coauthor of *Fully Present*

The

DHARMA

of

MODERN

MINDFULNESS

**Discovering the Buddhist Teachings
at the Heart of Mindfulness-Based
Stress Reduction**

BETH ANN MULLIGAN

New Harbinger Publications, Inc.

Publisher's Note

This publication is designed to provide accurate and authoritative information in regard to the subject matter covered. It is sold with the understanding that the publisher is not engaged in rendering psychological, financial, legal, or other professional services. If expert assistance or counseling is needed, the services of a competent professional should be sought.

Author's Note

In the stories of the "participants" in this book, all names and identifying features have been changed. In many cases they are composites of several people. The confidentiality of all participants has been honored and maintained.

Distributed in Canada by Raincoast Books

Copyright © 2017 by Beth Ann Mulligan
        New Harbinger Publications, Inc.
        5674 Shattuck Avenue
        Oakland, CA 94609
        www.newharbinger.com

Cover design by Amy Shoup

Acquired by Jess O'Brien

Edited by Ken Knabb

All Rights Reserved

Library of Congress Cataloging-in-Publication Data on file

19   18   17

10   9   8   7   6   5   4   3   2   1   First Printing

To Hugh Columba O'Neill
You shine your goodness on everything—like the sun.

And to the peace of all beings everywhere,
without any exception.

CONTENTS

FOREWORD

Beth Mulligan lives in three worlds. As a medical professional, she functions as a healer and companion to people in physical distress. As a Zen practitioner, she has committed herself to discovering the illuminating truth that lies hidden in the midst of this mysterious life of birth, suffering, and death. And as a teacher of Mindfulness-Based Stress Reduction (MBSR), she teaches ordinary people to find a new relationship to their physical, mental, and emotional suffering.

In this book, Beth finds a way to show us how her three worlds interconnect. Through stories and teachings, she brings us all into her own heart-mind as she teaches an eight-week MBSR program, all the while living her life in the mountains and desert and working as a physician assistant in a busy medical clinic. Like all MBSR teachers, she avoids the use of explicit Buddhist teachings and language in her guidance of her MBSR students. But in her writing, she lets us see her mind and helps us understand one of the primary roots of MBSR—the classical teachings of Buddhism.

I first met Jon Kabat-Zinn in 1992, when I was a young mother and wife, a psychotherapist, and a student of Zen. I hadn't been able to find a way to combine these different aspects of my life up until that point. Sitting in Jon's MBSR class at the Stress Reduction Clinic at the University of Massachusetts in Worcester, Massachusetts, I found myself in tears. He had discovered a way to touch the hearts of all the people in the class who had come seeking some kind of a fix for their troubles, which were many and varied. I was lucky to find a home at the Clinic, teaching MBSR classes. Under Jon's successor as executive director of the Center for Mindfulness, Saki Santorelli, I eventually became assistant director of the Clinic and a director of the professional training program, guiding professionals to learn to teach MBSR.

When Beth came to the Center to take one of these teacher trainings, I immediately recognized the depth of her practice, her capacity to bring everything to her learning, and her endearing lack of pretense. Beth doesn't put on airs or act like she is anything but a regular person. This quality comes through vividly in her book.

After twenty amazing years, I left the University to focus on my Zen practice and teaching. But what I learned from Jon, Saki, and my many mentors and friends at the Center has strongly influenced how I teach Zen: a deep respect for people just as they are, and the capacity to use ordinary language to communicate the teachings of Zen and Buddhism without relying on jargon or foreign words.

It feels important to repeat that Buddhism—Buddhist words and teachings—are never mentioned in an MBSR class. But for a teacher of MBSR, knowing something about these classic teachings is quite important. As Beth says, Jon Kabat-Zinn didn't invent mindfulness. No one did. The capacity to be present in each moment is something that everyone has from the beginning. The Buddha was just a person who discovered what it was like to live in this awakened way. Jon created a program that combines these ancient teachings with modern discoveries in psychology, neuroscience, stress physiology, and medicine—and in a plain, uncluttered language. And now Beth has given us the gift of this book, so that you can experience these teachings for yourself. Enjoy!

—Melissa Myozen Blacker, Roshi
Abbot and Guiding Teacher,
Boundless Way Zen

INTRODUCTION

Many Streams, One River

A group of people of diverse ages and cultural backgrounds sit in a circle in a hospital conference room together. Some are on chairs, one is in a wheelchair, and some sit on round cushions on the floor. They are very still and quiet. It's almost as if they are breathing together like a single organism. What are they doing? Or not doing? Is anyone the leader or teacher? It's hard to tell. A siren wails outside, no one stirs. A few minutes later the distinctive rhythmic sound of a "Medivac" helicopter is heard overhead. Someone will soon be taken to the E.R. and surrounded by busy focused people. Just a few hours ago I was one of those busy people, rushing down the hospital corridor to attend to a patient in the ICU. What you can't see is that in the silence of this circle, we are radiating our good will: wishing well to ourselves, each other, the people in the hospital, our friends and families, and all living beings.

After thirty minutes I ring a bell. Eyes open, arms lift to stretch, and there are some smiles as the people look around the room and catch each other's eyes. This is the final class—the final moments of an eight-week Mindfulness-Based Stress Reduction program (hereafter referred to as MBSR). These thirty people have been on a journey together, even an adventure. These folks have *been through* something together, it's palpable. Just a short while ago many words of appreciation were spoken, and stories of transformation were told, and now we sit for a few lingering minutes acknowledging our shared journey, though in an unusual way—without words, simply basking in quiet gratitude for each other.

At the beginning of this eight-week program, you would have known right away that I was the teacher. I had a clipboard and I checked folks in as they entered. I welcomed them and handed them class materials. I led us in an opening meditation. Then I talked—quite a lot. I described the MBSR program to them (as I soon will for you, dear reader). However, as each of the eight weeks has gone by, I speak less and less and the teachings come from anywhere and everywhere in the circle. This is the quintessential form of MBSR: what the founder of this program, Jon Kabat-Zinn, calls "inside-out" or experiential learning. This mode of learning is found also at places where Buddhist teachings are shared. Everyone becomes their own and each other's teacher, as we practice this stillness and silence, called meditation, together. Even though I am the teacher, I am also being taught by the students repeatedly—taught that relief from suffering is possible and that we are all wise and whole.

When the idea of this book came into being, I knew right away how to go about writing it. I would invite you into one of my MBSR classes, into the clinic where I practice medicine, and into the Dharma centers where I study and teach Buddhist meditation, and let the participants tell you about their understanding of the Dharma of MBSR. Here, Dharma is defined as the Buddha's timeless teachings on the nature of reality.

Linda: Student and Teacher

Ten years ago Linda entered the very conference room mentioned above, using a special walker that she could maneuver with one hand while the other arm was in sling. The walker had a pouch in the front in which sat her bright-eyed service dog, a small white poodle named Kiki. While Kiki looked me square in the eye, as if to say, "What are you going to do to my person?" Linda's eyes were cast down as she looked around nervously for a place to sit. I approached her, greeted her, and helped her get situated. She sighed. "It's really stressful coming to this stress-reduction program. But then everything is stressful."

"I know it is, Linda, and I appreciate your efforts to be here," I said.

I had met Linda at the orientation session where folks from the community come to learn about MBSR. What I knew about her was that she had recently moved to the southern California desert from Seattle, where she had been an engineer, highly positioned in a tech company. In the last year she had come down with a complex neurological disorder that could not be easily diagnosed or treated. She suffered from seizures, chronic pain, and frequent falls. She could not take care of herself.

When we met last week she told me, "I've pretty much lost everything. My career, my work in social action, my partner, and my tennis, which was like a religion to me. I am in incredible pain physically and emotionally. I am undergoing clinical trials at the Mayo Clinic, but I want to take as much of this class as I can. It's my last resort. Do you think it can help me?"

"I think this is an important question, one that we might explore together over the next eight weeks," I replied. "I try not to make guarantees, but I have seen this program serve and transform many lives, lives of people in quite challenging situations, as you are in now. I feel it is worth a try." I paused for a moment, looking into her eyes. "It seems like you have a lot of courage and determination." She visibly brightened just for a moment, as if she had forgotten there was more to her than her disabilities.

If you've picked up this book, you may have some sense of what MBSR is and what Linda was about to embark on. If not, stick with me, I'm not only going to tell you about it, we're going to take the class together! I suspect that while you may not have had Linda's exact type of illness or losses, you have been touched by pain and grief in some form. Perhaps your suffering is the tremendous loss of a child or spouse, a great change in your finances, an overwhelming workload, or the pain of the planet itself. I suspect that you too have suffered and looked for answers, simply because you are human.

During the eight weeks of the class, Linda applied the same diligence she had used in her many fields of success prior to her illness. She found great peace in the meditation practices and began to relate to her situation differently. In the third class she said, "This week when I had a flare-up, instead of saying 'This is a bad day,' I found myself saying 'This is a bad moment,' and then later, 'This is a different day.' In fact, I am gradually replacing the words 'bad' or 'hard' with 'different.' It changes the way I feel about it."

By the end of the eight-week series, on the outside not much had changed. Linda was still undergoing diagnostic testing. She had not gotten her job, her partner, or her tennis back. She had had some reduction in her pain and less frequency of seizures, but beyond that, something had changed on the inside. She was at peace a great deal more of the time. "I'm starting to be okay with the life I have now, which eight weeks ago I didn't think was possible." Linda's relationship to her situation changed dramatically, through her participation in this program founded upon meditative practices. At the end she gave me an exquisite orchid that blooms twice a year, and whenever I see it I think, "Ah, Linda is blooming, too." We've stayed in touch all these years and so I know that she is.

Enter Jon Kabat-Zinn and MBSR

Many years ago I would not have had anything to offer a patient like Linda, other than temporary symptom relief and a kind ear, nor would my colleagues in health care. We would certainly not have been able to prescribe something that would offer her the ability to live a peaceful life without being able to cure or fix her. Then, in 1979, Jon Kabat-Zinn, a molecular biologist and long-time meditation practitioner in the Buddhist tradition, with a committed yoga practice as well, created something quite different, something that could offer this possibility. He had found incredible value in his own daily meditation practice. He also worked in a busy medical center. Talking with the physicians there, he was surprised to find out that they felt they only really helped about 20 percent of their patients. "What happens to everyone else?" he asked. They replied, "Well, some get better on their own, and the rest fall into this chronic limbo where we really can't help them very much."

Kabat-Zinn realized that meditation and yoga might be beneficial for these patients with hard-to-treat chronic conditions who were "falling through the cracks" of the health care system. These patients were very unlikely to go to a Buddhist center or even a yoga class. But they could perhaps be challenged to do something for themselves that no one else on the planet, including their doctors or surgeons, could do for them— to learn meditation as a vital component to the medical care they were receiving, not a substitute for it. The idea was to offer meditation training based on the cultivation of mindfulness right in the heart of the medical center. It would be fairly rigorous, but there would be no beliefs or doctrines, no religion offered, but simply ancient, time-tested practices in a group format that he hoped would offer relief.

In his wisdom, Kabat-Zinn took the Pali word *dukkha* (Pali being the original language of the Buddha), usually translated as "suffering," and translated it with the somewhat less intimidating term, "stress." He went on to create a program designed to "reduce stress," a notion that most contemporary people can relate to quite easily. This allowed him to cast the net of support as widely as possible.

Kabat-Zinn developed the program into an eight-week curriculum and named it "Mindfulness-Based Stress Reduction." It includes intensive training in meditative practices, mindful movement based on yoga, educational components of stress physiology, creative responding to stressful situations, and bringing awareness to many areas of life, including communication, relationships, and making healthy choices.

Word about the program spread through Jon's best-selling book, *Full Catastrophe Living*, first published in 1990, and the PBS special, *Healing and the Mind*, which first aired in 1993. This documentary, which follows Bill Moyers and a group of patients at UMASS Medical Center through the eight-week program, informed millions of people—including me—about MBSR. In the decades since its inception, evidence-based research shows that MBSR not only helps people anecdotally, but has many measurable benefits, demonstrating improvements in chronic pain, depression, anxiety, and immune function, to mention just a few of the known benefits.

Professional training for health professionals became available through the UMASS Center for Mindfulness, producing more MBSR teachers and allowing more and more people from all walks of life to have access to MBSR. It is taught in many languages, in many countries and cultures. It is helping someone right this very moment. You might be one of these people.

The MBSR Door and the Dharma Door

Two weeks after her MBSR program ended, Linda called me and said she wanted to learn more about the origins of these practices that had helped her so much. Could I help her delve into the teachings of the Buddha? The request isn't one I often get—most people are content to stick with the original MBSR program, which serves them well enough through sustained practice for a lifetime. But for some folks there is also a curiosity about one of the ancient wisdom traditions this modern program was founded on: the Buddha's teaching. When that happens, I support the student as I did with Linda, inviting her to come and practice at the Insight Buddhist Center in Palm Springs where I teach. I also suggested some books, and on her own she found a teacher, a Buddhist nun who worked with her one-on-one.

She became a regular at the Center, and even volunteered at special events. When the idea of this book came up, I thought Linda would be great person to talk with. While I have my own sense of the value of the Buddhist underpinnings of MBSR and what the Dharma offers me, I wanted to get a feel for what these ancient teachings could mean to a wider audience, and how it might transform their suffering in other ways. So I asked her, "What, if anything, did exploring the teachings of the Buddha add to your practice, or to your life?"

"It helped me put my suffering in a bigger container," she said succinctly. I thought I knew what she meant, but I asked her to say a little more.

"You know the story about the salt?" she asked.

"Tell me," I said.

"There was a student of the Buddha who despite years of practice suffered terribly. One day, after trying many other things, the Buddha told him to take a teaspoon of salt in a glass of water and drink it down. 'How did it taste?' the Buddha asked. 'Very salty,' said the student. 'Now,' said the Buddha, 'put it in this large jug. How does it taste now?' 'Not so salty,' said the student. 'And now,' said the Buddha, 'put the salt in the stream here and drink from the stream.' The student did as instructed and his suffering was alleviated, he became free. That is what continuing on the path of the Buddha has done with me and my condition. The stream for me is seeing my wholeness and the whole of humanity."

"Thank you," I said. "That's so helpful. Is there anything else?"

"Yes. A lot. You might be sorry you asked! The teachings offer more space not only around my suffering, but also around who I thought I was. I used to think my value was in my academic degrees and my work, in my home, and in my partner, in having an athletic body and being strong all the time. At first, when I lost all of that I didn't know who I was. I felt like nothing. What's happened over time is that I've seen that I am much more than those things and I'm not defined by any of them or by my illness. Do you know how that happened?"

"Please tell me."

"On the first night of class, you *saw* me. You said I was courageous and determined to be there, and I felt like a door opened where I was so closed down around my illness. I've had this experience with you and my other teacher many times—when I could not see myself, you saw me until I could. I also appreciate the teachings on ethics and the connection to our hearts through the teachings on loving-kindness. To be honest, Beth, those were missing from my life even before I became ill. I had lost a connection to my deepest values and to my capacity to care, in my drive to succeed and in my constant busyness. I wouldn't call myself a Buddhist, but I love the teachings and am grateful for the path. I would say MBSR and the Buddha's teachings are two of many streams leading to one river."

This time spent with Linda over a cup of tea told me exactly what I needed to know to write this book. Many people like myself came to MBSR through the "Dharma door"—that is, we were Buddhist practitioners long before we learned about the riches of this contemporary program. When we did discover MBSR, it seemed like a skillful vehicle to offer relief to people who might not want to, or be able to, come through the "Dharma door." And the flip side is when I teach MBSR to Buddhist practitioners and they say, "I learned so much through the connection to my body. I learned how to apply my practice in everyday life in a way I never saw before."

I found the MBSR door in 1995 when I saw the Bill Moyers PBS documentary *Healing and the Mind*. At the time I had been practicing medicine as a board-certified physician assistant since my graduation from the Duke P.A. program in 1982. I had also been practicing meditation and yoga to address my own suffering since I was a teenager. Growing up in a complicated and alcoholic family, with its attendant violence and neglect, I had experienced much suffering, particularly feeling worthless and alone. I came to practice desperately looking for peace and for connection.

Through the suggestion of a friend, I found the teachings of Thich Nhat Hanh. I sat my first retreat with him, and after a week in silence with him, his monks and nuns, and hundreds of other sincere practitioners, I tasted a freedom that captured my heart and gave me a glimpse of the possibility that I might actually be okay. This set me on the Buddha's path, which I have continued to follow to this very day. For years my meditation and yoga practice and my professional medical practice existed side by side. Now it seemed possible that they could hold hands.

When I saw the documentary, watching patients who looked much like my own, in a medical center that also looked familiar, doing meditation and yoga to "heal from within," as the segment was called, these two worlds came together for me in a powerful way. I was riveted and inspired. The program awakened in me a deep yearning to serve my patients the way I had been served, through the ancient practices that had transformed my own suffering. In the subsequent years, after much professional training in teaching MBSR, I have seen this possibility flower into a reality in my local hospital and its adjoining cancer center, as well as in neighborhood schools, universities, and nonprofit organizations. I also now offer it at the Dharma center where I am Guiding Teacher, but I don't mention the Buddha or use any Dharma language. I teach the curriculum as is. Many streams, one river. Each stream gives life in its own right and needs no supplement. But still there is that river...

MBSR and the Two Zeros

Several years ago, at a retreat held for teachers of mindfulness-based interventions taught by Jon Kabat-Zinn and long-time Dharma teacher Christina Feldman, Christina shared this story with us: "Recently an article appeared in an English newspaper about mindfulness. It was titled 'Mindfulness in a Raisin' and began with the sentence: 'Twenty-five years ago an American scientist invented mindfulness.' I wrote to the editor about their somewhat sloppy journalism. They forgot two zeros. Mindfulness comes from a tradition which is at least twenty-five hundred years old." While soft laughter rippled through the room, something important was being illuminated here. I felt it and knew it, and it became something I thought about for years after. It may have been the seed that sprouted this book: *What about the two zeros? What might we find at the joining of the two streams?*

The Buddha's Story, Our Story

The story of a man known as Siddhartha Gautama (his family name) or the Buddha (his spiritual name, meaning "the awakened one"), who is estimated to have lived about 2,500 years ago, has captured the hearts and minds of millions of people through the ages to this very day. Why? The Buddha's story, his life, his struggles, and his path to freedom, is one that many people from varying cultures, ages, and backgrounds can relate to. Let me tell you some of his story and see if it resonates in any way for you.

Scholars say that Siddhartha grew up in India around 500–600 BCE. Born into a royal family, he was intentionally protected from the difficulties and challenges of this earthly human life by his father. Siddhartha grew restless and curious about the world that existed beyond the palace walls, just as we too may have had a period where we had to find out if there was something in life other than the family, the cultural conditioning, and the society we grew up in.

Siddhartha's curiosity led him to leave the palace compound with his charioteer and to plunge into the wild street life of India, where he quickly encountered all aspects of the human condition. It is said that he saw a sick person for the first time, then an old person, and then a corpse. He repeatedly asked his companion, "What has happened to this person, and will it happen to me?" Each time, the charioteer answered him truthfully, "This person is ill, and yes, to have a human body is to experience sickness, and to age; and all living beings will die." This came as a shock to the protected prince. These aspects of being human may be shocking to us as well.

On this outing Siddhartha also encountered a "holy man" or monk with a look of peace and great composure on his face, in the midst of all of the chaos and calamities. He wondered if he, too, could learn to live peacefully in the face of these harsh realities. He wanted to have what he saw on the monk's face.

After witnessing life's stark realities, Siddhartha left his father's home and royal responsibilities and spent six years practicing the spiritual traditions of the time in order to attain that monk's peace. This included the use of physical depriva-tion and extreme self-denials to try to "transcend" the physical body. It is said that during this time he was living on one grain of rice a day, and this deprivation showed in his body—you could see his vertebrae through his abdomen. These practices produced altered or mystical states of consciousness. Siddhartha grew so adept at reaching these states that he amassed a band of followers, but these states only lasted for a while and did not definitively answer his compelling questions: "How may I live with dignity and peace in the face of suffering?"

Temporary Fix or Lasting Peace?

We find ourselves in similar circumstances today. At the time MBSR came into being, the practice of medicine was (and actually still is) mainly focused on treating symptoms of dis-eases with what are often temporary fixes. It often does not get down to the root causes of what may be driving an illness. And so it is with our lives in general. Like Siddhartha, prior to coming to MBSR people have tried many pathways to heal what ails them. But we often do not get down to the root causes of our problems—or to any insight about how we can live with dignity despite what ails us (as Linda did through MBSR).

Rather than leading to enlightenment, Siddhartha's prac-tices weakened him so badly that one day he fell into a river and almost drowned. A young woman goat herder, Sujata, saw him, pulled him out of the water, and offered him some rice and milk. Gradually regaining his strength, Siddhartha began to question the path he'd been following. He was deeply struck by the natural compassion of this ordinary woman, who was not trained in any spiritual path. Perhaps, he thought, there is some natural way of being, something already in us that can be cultivated without starvation and extremism. He already knew it was not found in the life of luxury. He had a memory of being a young boy sitting under the shade of a rose apple tree, watching a festival, and feeling content and complete. He began to wonder if sitting still and allowing the mind to focus in a relaxed way on what was right in front of him would enable him to find what he'd been looking for.

Determined to awaken to this natural contentment, compassion, and understanding, he stopped everything he was doing and simply sat under a tree. One day, after several days of nonstop sitting, he looked up and saw the morning star and realized something clear and true: we are already awake and whole—"all beings and the great earth," he said, "not just me." Or in the words of Jon Kabat-Zinn (and this is an essential theme of MBSR): "As long as you are breathing, there is more right with you than wrong with you, no matter what is 'wrong.'"

People come to MBSR with these same questions, much like Linda did, asking, "How can I live peacefully with this challenge?" What brings *you* to this practice, to this book? What hardships of the human condition are you experiencing? It could be as simple as not being able to sleep well at night due to the intense stress of your job, or as difficult as the drug addiction of your teenage child. Whatever it is that you are facing, like Siddhartha you want to know how to live in peace.

Taking Our Seat—A Radical Act

For Siddhartha (hereafter referred to as the Buddha), taking his seat under that tree was a radical act, one that reverberates throughout time. He committed to look within, to thoroughly examine his own experience and to see what truth and freedom could be realized through this investigation. In the same way, when people come to MBSR, they are in fact taking this radical act of taking their seat, a front row seat on their own lives. They are breaking free from the tendency to look outside for answers, for ways to escape the human condition—an even stronger pull now, perhaps, than in the Buddha's time. In MBSR we turn inward, honoring and rediscovering the wholeness already present in all of us. In the first week, participants are invited to lie down for forty-five minutes and spend that time simply visiting all the parts of their own body with the teacher's guided instructions. There is a rich learning environment here, in the body, if we only knew it. These discoveries are some of what we'll explore in the stories of participants in the subsequent chapters.

Mindfulness Methods and Medicine

There are some unique features about the way the Buddha offered his teachings. For instance, he did not offer a particular doctrine or dogma, but rather asked people to accept a teaching "only when it agrees with your experience and reason, and when it is conducive to the good and gain of oneself and all others." In MBSR, teachers approach the class similarly. We offer practices in a safe environment, practices which allow participants to access their own inner wisdom. There is very little written material, very little reading, and most of the homework and the class time are spent engaging in meditative practices and then reflecting on what has come up in those practices. We learn together.

So how does someone like myself, trained in medicine, with years of diagnosing, prescribing medication and therapeutic regimes, trained to fix, offer answers, or refer to specialists, face someone like Linda and not offer suggestions? Reading a book on Buddhism, or even attending a great teacher training, would not give me the confidence to do this. What gives me the faith and confidence is the same thing that my teachers have: my own transformative experiences on (and off) the cushion. A prerequisite to becoming an MBSR teacher is that one has an established personal meditation practice and has sat numerous multiday silent retreats.

In an article Jon Kabat-Zinn wrote on the origins of MBSR, he says, "Mindfulness can only be understood from the inside out. It is not one more cognitive-behavioral technique to be deployed in a behavior change paradigm, but a way of being and a way of seeing that has profound implications for understanding the nature of our own minds and bodies, and for living life as if it really mattered." And you know what? It does really matter. In other words, you have to practice!

Most of my retreat experiences have been in the Zen tradition. A Zen retreat has a rigorous schedule, with many periods of silent sitting meditation, walking meditation, and working meditation. There are Dharma talks once a day, and many opportunities to meet one-on-one with the teacher. But most of what happens is in the silence of one's own practice. Here I learned to hold myself, to stand by myself without "doing anything," watching knee pain come and go, heartbreak surface, overflow, and pass away, and joy arise while washing a pot.

At the end of these retreats there is a closing council. Each person is invited to share. Having sat through dozens of these, I am always struck by what has been happening in the silence and stillness and what remains at the end. Yes, people will say it was challenging, they thought they might not make it, they wanted to run out and buy a ham sandwich, but they end up filled with gratitude, compassion, and a feeling of deep connection with others. No one has instructed them explicitly in any of these wholesome qualities, although they are pointed to in the daily Dharma talks. They seem to arise naturally if we get out of the way. This is what the Buddha saw. This process is what allows us to offer this intentional non-doing to suffering people and watch in wonder as something changes. The Buddha said in multiple teachings, "I would not ask you to do this if I did not think you could do it." Now I am saying the same thing to you. You can do it. You just have to experience it for yourself.

The Wide Embrace of MBSR and the Buddha's Teachings

Buddhism and MBSR share a spirit of radical inclusiveness. Part of what the Buddha was known for was opening his teachings to all. Prior to him, the path to freedom was not available to everyone, but only to a few—to men of the Brahmin caste, the highest in society, and to people willing to give up everything and wander as a monk. The Buddha sought to teach anyone with a sincere desire to learn, anyone who sought to wake up and decrease suffering. It is said that he taught regular householders, including women, kings, beggars, thieves, prostitutes, and ordinary tradespeople. MBSR has had a similar inclusiveness effect in our time, bringing mindfulness practices out of the temple and into the places where we live, work, and play.

You very definitely don't need to be a Buddhist to take or teach MBSR, or other contemporary non-Buddhist courses on mindfulness. That is not the intention of this book. In fact, the Buddha wasn't a Buddhist! He was a man who saw clearly into the nature of reality, who saw a path to freedom and shared his realizations with anyone who was interested. His invitation stays open with no strings attached. So does mine. I invite you to join me on an adventure, and to see if there is a facet of learning about the Dharma that may, as in Linda's case, connect you to the jewels of your values and your heart. I trust that you, like so many others over the centuries, will find that the best teacher is the practice; and that through practice, and through ancient and modern teachings and stories, you'll find the wisdom that lies within your own heart; and that the best teacher is you. Whatever stream feeds you, my wish is that this book will allow you to place your suffering in a much bigger container: the river that is as big as the whole universe.

Each chapter will take you into the MBSR classroom, where we can listen to the inner wisdom of the students, week by week. In some chapters you will be directed to a particular practice. I've developed guided audios you can download for many of the practices in this book. There are also guided reflections, intentions, and practices for each chapter to support your personal exploration of the teachings. All these materials are available at the website for this book: www.newharbinger .com/39164. (See the very back of this book for information on how to access this content.)

A NOTE ABOUT THE
SPIRIT OF THIS BOOK

MBSR has several foundational elements that inform the curriculum. These include: experiential education, stress psychology and physiology, neuroscience, non-dual wisdom traditions, and teaching and practices from Buddhism. This book primarily focuses on the Buddhist underpinnings, not because they are more important , but because it is one lens, the one in which I am best versed, through which we may look at MBSR. You will see the other foundations implicitly woven throughout the book.

It was never a secret that Dr. Kabat-Zinn, the creator of Mindfulness-Based Stress Reduction, practiced Buddhist meditation and based much of MBSR's curriculum, and particularly its practices, on these ancient teachings. He was, however, skillful and careful in translating the teachings into modern language, very intentionally *not* including Pali or Sanskrit terms or referring to the Buddha in the curriculum, so as to serve as many people as possible from all walks of life. The wisdom of this approach has proved its worth: millions of people have benefited from this curriculum who might not have if it were presented in any other way.

As mindfulness becomes ever more popular, moving from medical journals to *The Wall Street Journal*, *Oprah*, a cover story in *Time* magazine, and a segment on *60 Minutes*, many of us who teach and practice mindfulness feel moved to reconnect the concept of mindfulness to its roots—to the "two zeros" I mentioned in the Introduction and what they represent. Otherwise, this now-ubiquitous term "mindfulness" may seem like simply a way to train attention and to increase performance and productivity. It can even seem like one more thing we might do or buy. Without some understanding of the two zeros, the foundations of ethics and heartfulness might be lost. I've heard Jon Kabat-Zinn say, "When I say mindfulness, I'm saying it with a capital M, meaning the whole Dharma."

Before embarking on this book, I talked the subject over with Jon Kabat-Zinn and received his support for discussing aspects of the Dharma that are embedded in MBSR. I proposed to do this strictly from my personal experience, in the context of an MBSR "class" that is a composite of some of the many classes I have taught over the years. Not as a scholar or expert, because I am not either one. The eight-week course, and my experience teaching it, has turned out to be a really fruitful framework for me to explore connections between Dharma concepts and the journey of MBSR. I am not in any way trying to say that Dr. Kabat-Zinn put this specific teaching in class 1, or class 2, or class 8. It's simply how I see it from my teaching and practitioner perspective.

Buddhism, as a tradition of wisdom and practice, spread from India all across Asia and eventually to the West. Each country and culture has added its own flavor to his teachings, and there are many different types of practices depending on what country you are in. So there isn't just one Buddhism, although there is a lot of overlap. For example, Tibetan Buddhism might look very different from Japanese or Zen Buddhism. So when I say we'll explore the Buddhist underpinnings in MBSR, I have chosen to focus on some foundational and essential teachings that are found in all of the many branches. Mainly the Four Noble Truths (which include the Eightfold Path) and the Four Foundations of Mindfulness. Please see the "Recommended Readings and Resources" at the end of the book, which I drew on in the writing of this book and use to support my personal practice.

All that being said, it remains important to those of us who teach MBSR that we continue to refrain from using Buddhist terminology in our classes. So if you are new to teaching MBSR or are on a pathway, please don't use any of the Dharma language in this book in your classes. If you find the Buddhist perspective useful, practice and explore it for yourself and its benefits will come through you and be sensed by others, even if you are not using the terminology. This protects the inclusiveness originally intended by Jon Kabat-Zinn and allows MBSR to continue to benefit thousands of people every year as they learn to embrace the whole of themselves and their lives.

Chapter 1

THE DHARMA OF SUFFERING:
It's Not Personal

It's the end of a long day of patient care and I have hung up my white coat and red stethoscope on the old wooden coat rack in my office. There are only two charts left on the counter, a miracle! I will tackle them tomorrow. I pick up my purse and a small red cooler with my dinner in it and head for the front door.

"Teaching tonight?" the receptionist Chris asks.

"Yes. How about you—soccer with the girls?" She has two granddaughters she is devoted to.

"No, tonight is swimming."

"Have fun, and thanks for everything. Today wasn't the easiest."

She smiles. "See you tomorrow."

I get in my old Honda and drive twenty minutes east to the medical center in Palm Desert where I will teach my regular Thursday night MBSR class. This evening is class 1 of a new series. I keep the car quiet so I can start to let go of all I have seen, felt, and heard today. Twenty-four patients, all with bodies and stories of challenges and suffering.

I've been seeing patients for a very long time, since I was twenty-five years old, fresh out of Duke's physician assistant program and into my first job in the basement clinic of Los Angeles County Hospital. Now I work in a small but busy managed-care practice that serves groups like public school teachers, the folks who clean and tend the gardens of the local hotels, the older population on Medicare, and local families. My job is to try to diagnose and treat what is ailing them. Sometimes I can and often I can't. While I received great training in physical examination, diagnosis, and treatment, no one ever spoke about the enormous amount of suffering I would encounter in the practice of medicine. Once the exam door opens, the full scope of what it is to be human—with all the sorrows and joys of this life—also opens. I may find myself sitting with someone who just lost a daughter, a husband, a job, or her health. Every single day in my practice I encounter what the Buddha called "the First Noble Truth": the fact of suffering. Suffering, he taught, was one of the conditions of the human experience.

In my early years I focused mainly on the physical findings with my patients. We talked about diseases and treatments; we rarely talked about broken hearts or loss. It was all I knew how to do. Later, as I learned about the Buddha's teachings and, most importantly, developed a personal meditation practice, I was able to navigate these deep and difficult waters with more skill and awareness. I became more present to the whole person and tried to meet that person in his entire being, not just the body part or diagnosis. To meet his—our—suffering.

I arrive at the hospital education building, right next to the hospital itself. I take a moment to appreciate the green lawns and manmade ponds, a few ducks swimming around cheerfully. I need some time to transition from my day and my role as clinician—someone to whom patients look to for answers and someone who gives direct orders all day ("Take six units of insulin"; "Change your diet")—to teacher. Here I won't have answers and all of my suggestions will be much more in the invitational style we learn in our MBSR teacher training ("Taking your seat now when you're ready, and feeling your body in the chair").

I recognize that I am entering a realm of "not knowing" and a willingness to explore together as a partner with the participants, not as an expert.

I sit on the grass, take off my shoes, and feel the coolness on my feet. I eat my avocado sandwich slowly and reflect on the Dharma talk I heard on Sunday. Almost every Sunday you will find me sitting and practicing at Yokoji Zen Mountain Center. We do *zazen* (sitting meditation) together, listen to a talk together, eat together, and wash dishes together.

This past Sunday my teacher Tenshin Roshi gave a talk on "not knowing." Zen talks are usually formed around ancient dialogues between student and teacher or two students, called koans.

In this instance, Master Jizo asks his student Hogen, "Where are you going?"

Hogen replies, "I'm just wandering."

"Where are you wandering?"

"I don't know."

Master Jizo then says, "Not knowing is most intimate."

At that point Hogen attained enlightenment.

So as I face this new class, I remember that as many classes as I have taught, I don't know how this will go. This "not knowing" also invites us to be truly intimate with life, how it actually is in the moment rather than our ideas or perceptions about the moment. And while not knowing can be scary, it is also reality: anything can happen at any time. And not knowing can be more of an adventure! The other day I asked a young man serving me in Starbucks how he was and he said, "Same old, same old." It made me sad, though I can feel that way too if I am not really paying attention. So I enter the classroom with this spirit of Master Hogen.

I pull out my equipment for class—workbooks, CDs, a rolling bag with some yoga mats, and my teaching bag, with bells, poems, chapstick, and water bottle. This evening I will sit in a circle with another group of people. Here I have no white coat to protect me, no otoscope or scalpel, no prescription pads or test results. I won't be probing or prodding and I will make no attempt to diagnose or treat. It's just me, some meditation bells, a poem or two, time-tested practices, and the students. I know I will be meeting the universality of suffering here, too; with a somewhat different set of instruments, most of which are not visible. I have my practice, my teachers behind me, and a trust in the curriculum. As for the students, I've seen their names on the class roster, met them briefly at the orientation, and spoken with them. I've read their reasons for coming, I know the diagnoses and medications, but I don't them—yet.

As I finish arranging the room, a tall round woman with blonde hair wearing light blue scrubs approaches me. Trailing her is a young man who looks a lot like her, except for the spiky hair and tattoos on his arms.

"I'm Carol, the nurse from Labor and Delivery. We spoke on the phone."

"Hi, Carol, great to meet you, so glad you came. Please find a seat."

"Well, I brought my son. This is Zach." She draws me slightly away as he stares at the ceiling. "He has been through a really difficult time. He..." She chokes up. "Our family has had a lot of losses recently. And he is struggling very badly with depression. Nothing seems to be working and he is refusing to take medication. He's here as a sort of ultimatum, a last resort."

Oh dear, I think. That usually does not work. I normally would never let someone drag a family member unwillingly to the program. I pause and take a deep breath. What to do? "Well, in my experience," I say, "this kind of program, which is so participatory, only works for people who have some motivation to be here. So while I appreciate how much you want to help your son—after all, what could be more natural?—it's also important that you help yourself, which may in the long run help him. Also, if he doesn't want to be here..."

"I know, I know," she says. "But we're here."

"Yes, you are. Okay, why don't we try it for this one class and talk at the end."

Meanwhile the circle has filled with people of all ages, shapes, and sizes. Carol and Zach sit quite far apart from each other. Interestingly, he sits right next to my chair. We begin with a four-minute "arriving meditation." I acknowledge that sometimes the body arrives before the mind, and this might give us a chance to catch up with ourselves. I see smiles and nods. I invite everyone to take in the present moment with their eyes, seeing the shapes, colors, shadows of this room, with curiosity like a child might. And then to switch to hearing, and then feeling. That includes you! You might try this wherever you are right now. You can also access an audio of this exercise at www.newharbinger.com/39164 (Track 1: The GPS to the Present Moment).

Afterward I ask, "Did anyone notice any effect from this?"

"I feel a little calmer."

"I'm more 'here.'"

"It slowed me down."

"My mind was really busy even in that short time!"

What did you notice, dear reader? Whatever you experienced is okay. It's the noticing that's the practice.

My life and work partner Hugh O'Neill, MBSR teacher extraordinaire, calls this practice "the GPS to the present moment." Try it from time to time when you feel lost. It might be your way home.

I then give a brief overview of the eight-week program, emphasizing the courage it takes to come to a class that will require a bit of a leap into the unknown. After all, MBSR doesn't come in a bottle with a list of active ingredients. We also set up the conditions under which we will create a safe container for our journey together. That is: confidentiality, no cross talk or advice giving, and no need to fix one another. I know we will be meeting all kinds of suffering this evening; my intention is to create the classroom as a safe refuge.

At this point we go around the circle and people are invited to share their name, why they came, and what their hopes are.

"I'm caring for my husband, who has Alzheimer's. I'm worn out. I need a little time for myself and some tools so I can keep going," says an elegant woman with a pearl necklace named Renée.

"My name is Norma," says the next woman. "My husband has pancreatic cancer." She chokes. "The prognosis is not good. I worry all the time."

"I'm the husband," Alan says, looking down.

"I have three kids and a stressful job. I just feel angry all the time," says a young Latino man named Raúl. His wife is sitting next to him, she squeezes his arm affectionately. She says, "I'm Lisette. I've just been diagnosed with diabetes. I think it's due to stress."

And so around the circle it goes. We hear about chronic migraines, parents struggling with children's drug problems, aging, loss, back pain...until we get to the last person to my left—Zach.

"My mom dragged me here, honestly, it was an ultimatum. I didn't want to come. Listening to all of you, though, I feel for the first time in a long time that I am in the right place. I feel that you are my people. I have been through a really tough time, and I have been, well, pretty hopeless. Nothing has worked and I don't want to take meds. But right now I feel like I am in the right place." He nods vigorously, looking at everyone, his face wide open.

This was not what I was expecting. I am so moved it takes me a while to find any words. This is good, a bit of silence after such an honest statement doesn't need any embellishment.

Then into the silence Renée drops this: "I guess everyone has something."

It is as if a pearl from her necklace has been gently placed in the center of our circle. The crisp, clear, and compassionate truth of it sits there, shining and luminescent.

The First Noble Truth: We All Suffer

Renée isn't a Buddhist teacher or even a Buddhist practitioner. But she has just summed up one of the Buddha's core teachings. It's called the First Noble Truth. When the Buddha sat with his deep true question I mentioned in the Introduction, he came to this realization: there is suffering in this life. The word *dukkha* is the Pali word translated as suffering, or a feeling of dissatisfaction. By calling this a noble truth (or an ennobling truth), in a way, even before we even go any further, his statement is setting us free and it is in and of itself a kindness. Our suffering is not a sign of any sort of failure on our part, it simply is.

We can see this so clearly in Zach's response to listening to the circle of his fellow human beings, all suffering in different ways. Before, he felt alone, perhaps even singled out for hardship. Now he's recognized that he is part of the community of humans responding to the truth of suffering. He's had a glimpse of something he had not seen before. To realize that our suffering is not personal, although it can really feel that way, is wisdom.

Like Zach, many of us may feel isolated in our difficulties. Being ill, or caring for someone who is ill, is often a lonely situation. In our Western culture we may also get the idea that life is supposed to look like it does on television: people who are endlessly beautiful, thin, and happy. We look around, thinking that surely no one else feels this awkward, stupid, miserable, (fill in the blank). But when the Buddha said "there is suffering," he meant all of us.

Nowhere is the relief this realization can offer clearer than in the ancient story about a woman living in a village where the Buddha was teaching. Her baby had died. She was so grief-stricken that she carried the dead child in her arms, weeping inconsolably, and would not put him down. In desperation, she came to the Buddha and asked, "Could you please bring my son back to life?"

"I will," the Buddha replied. "But first you must go to every home in the village and bring me back a mustard seed from each home that has not been touched by death."

So she earnestly went from door to door. After circling the entire village, she came back to the Buddha with no mustard seeds, finally ready to release her son. She saw into the truth of suffering and the universality of death. And while it did not take her grief away, it gave her, perhaps, just enough peace to go on with her life.

The Three Refuges: Shelter from the Storm

The Buddha called sickness, old age, and death the heavenly messengers, because they can awaken us out of our trance of separation and set us on a path to freedom, as they did with him. Yes, he says, suffering is part of existence. But he doesn't leave us hanging there. As we'll see through the three other Noble Truths in subsequent chapters, there is a path leading to the relief of suffering.

There is also a way to get help anywhere, any time. This is called "taking refuge." When it rains, we find shelter, right? The Buddhist shelter from the downpours of life is what are called the Three Refuges: the Buddha, the Dharma, and the Sangha. One way of looking at the first refuge is that we can take comfort in the historical figure of the Buddha, in the fact that such a wise, enlightened being existed, whose teachings are here to help us. Another way to see this is, we can take refuge in the awareness that we too have our own capacities to wake up, our own wisdom and awareness. The second refuge is the Dharma, again seen in two ways: the teachings of the Buddha—the path of practice the Buddha offered to relieve our suffering—*and* the teachings that are available to us everywhere, from our own lives. The third shelter is the Sangha, the community of spiritual friends—the people traveling the path along with you, the people you can count on in your life.

People come to an MBSR program seeking refuge from all manner of human suffering. As you can see in our group above, it's everything from work stress to terminal illness. In your life you too have many stressors and challenges. Are you seeking a true refuge? We all seek what might be called "false refuges," the quick things that take the edge off—alcohol, food (usually number one these days, when I ask), drugs (both prescribed and not), technological distraction, and overwork, to name a few.

In MBSR we begin to find a more reliable and nonharmful refuge in our own awake and aware nature. After all, the word "Buddha" isn't the guy's name, it means awake! I often point out to my new students that it shows a great deal of awareness just to choose to come to a program that offers an invisible solution, a solution that involves sitting or lying still and being willing to look at one's own experience, no matter how difficult. Taking refuge in the Buddha in this context means we can trust our own capacity to hold our difficulties courageously. We can trust ourselves.

In MBSR classes we can take refuge in the fact that we all know the truth of reality when we hear, feel, taste, touch, or see it. When Renée says, "I guess everyone has something," we can all take solace in the truth of that. That is taking refuge in the Dharma.

Going around the circle after the guidelines for creating safe and confidential sharing are established, we create Sangha, community. And even on the first night we saw—again through Zach's eyes—how powerfully healing that can be.

Mindfulness in a Raisin

After we've gone around sharing what brings us here, I place two raisins in each person's hands and ask them to see these objects as if they don't know what they are. "Imagine you are visiting from another planet and you have to make a report to the "Mother Ship." People call out adjectives of their visual impression: "wrinkled," "oval," "irregular," "golden." Then we smell them, feel them, listen to them, and finally place one in our mouth, noticing all that goes on with the tongue and salivary glands even before we start chewing and the burst of flavor comes forth. It's an exploration of something we do every day— eating. But we do it in a particular way that transforms the experience for most people. I used to be a bit apprehensive about this, because it seems silly or awkward to some people. But actually most people engage, and even more interestingly, they learn something. After it's over, I ask, "How is to eat a raisin like that? How do you feel?"

"Peaceful."

"Grateful."

"Weird, it stuck to my teeth."

"Connection."

"Awkward."

"I noticed I wasn't thinking about anything."

"I noticed I want more."

"Funny, I was actually surprised at how satisfied I am with just two."

They are teaching the class already.

From what I understand about the MBSR curriculum, the raisin-eating practice is placed here right at the beginning of our journey to invite people to bring the awareness that we use in formal meditative practices to something ordinary and familiar. It's here to help us see that meditation isn't something strange that must be done in a certain posture, but rather a way of paying attention that is readily available, that can be done quite easily and naturally in a wide variety of settings. "This," we say, "*is* meditation." Later, when we ask participants to feel the breath, we can refer back to this experience as "breathing with curiosity—the way you tasted the raisin."

The raisin practice embodies the "inside-out learning" that Jon Kabat-Zinn spoke about, as well as the Buddha's teaching to directly experience the path. We don't give a lecture on dropping out of automatic pilot; we actually drop out of it. If you have taken an MBSR class or perhaps visited a Dharma center, you know that every session begins with a period of silent meditational practice, before any verbal teaching. In this way you can see if what is being taught is real for you. The curriculum is the experience and the awareness of the experience.

After the raisin practice, I tell folks we are going to do a guided meditation, the "body scan." This is usually done lying down, but may also be done in a chair. I will explain it in more detail in the next chapter, but you can access an audio of this exercise at www.newharbinger.com/39164 (Track 2: The Body Scan).

"We're going to be spending some time visiting our own bodies and asking what we feel moment to moment," I explain. "No particular way to feel, simply bringing curiosity to what is here. In a way you could say we're going to explore our bodies with the same spirit of the raisin."

I lie down and show them my favorite position, the "astronaut's pose": all of me on the floor but my calves draped over the chair seat like an upside-down astronaut. While people are adjusting and finding their spots, a woman named Jean comes over to me and leans over. She's been glaring at me most of the session. "I need you to know, my body hurts all over, all the time," she says. "I don't see how I am going to do this."

I prop myself up on one elbow to get eye contact. "Jean, that sounds truly challenging. And I realize this sounds counterintuitive, but would you be willing to try it? Do the best you can and feel free to use anything that you already know will help you." Surprisingly, she goes quietly to her spot and sets up a number of cushions and pillows while I breathe with awareness of my anxiety and calm myself.

At the end of the meditation, I ring the bell and ask the participants to take their time sitting up. People always look a bit different after the body scan, a little softer, sleepier for sure.

Jean sits up and looks at me, but it is not a glare and her voice is more resonant. "I learned something!"

"Oh?" (*Oh God*, I think…)

"My body doesn't hurt all over and it doesn't hurt all the time. There are parts that don't hurt and some of the other really bad parts, well, they change a bit." She actually smiles.

Jean has been paying careful attention!

Okay, I'll admit it, I'm kind of jumping up and down inside. Mind you, it doesn't always go this way, this isn't a fairy tale, and I've heard it go the other way many times. As in "My body hurts way more than I ever imagined!" But this is a true story, folks, and it is something to celebrate, if only for a fleeting moment. This is the true Dharma, seeing for oneself the actual experience rather than our painful story *about* the experience.

What about you? Are there moments when your felt experience doesn't match your thoughts about it? Or times when they do?

There isn't time for a lot of discussion during this class, but I assign the class homework: practice the body scan six days this week; eat one meal, or part of one, mindfully; and try practicing mindfulness of other daily activities. I suggest that they choose something specific, like washing their hands (this is a great one I do with health care providers), driving, gardening, cooking, even feeling the doorknob when you enter the house.

"Feel the water on your skin as you shower," I say, "noticing if you're already mentally at work, and then bringing the attention to the sensation of the water, the smell of the soap. Or you might try it while preparing food, smelling the first slice of a tomato. Or try mindful driving, feeling the steering wheel under your hands, the seat behind your back, seeing the colors and shapes around you."

I stand at the door and say farewell to the students. Zach and Carol linger.

"I'd really like to take the class, Beth." Zach says. "For me."

"I'm glad, Zach. I'll see you next week."

Carol gives me a hug, a hard one. And they leave. *This not knowing is most intimate*, I think. How could I have known what would transpire in this one class, with this one young man who just dropped in—well, maybe with a little push from his mom. And yet here we are in this intimate moment.

Chapter 2

THE DHARMA OF THE BODY: What We Resist Persists

This afternoon as I drive to the medical center, I am thinking about a new student I am going to meet before class. The MBSR program is offered through a branch of the hospital called the Center for Healthy Living, run by two wonderful women, Sandra and Louise, who truly support the MBSR program and championed it within the medical center. On Monday I got a call from Louise that her husband was in serious trouble. "Brian had a hip replacement three months ago, and it didn't take. He developed an infection and nothing seems to be working. They took the hardware out and now they're trying to get it cleaned out enough so he can have another surgery. But meanwhile he has just completely fallen apart. We know your class has already started, but I don't know what else to do! He cries all the time and then I cry and my kids are beside themselves. The antidepressants seemed to make him worse..." The words cascaded out of her in a rush.

"Oh, Louise, I'm so sorry, how incredibly difficult for you all. Please ask him to meet me at six o'clock and I'll see what I can do."

I arrive to class early and outside the classroom on a bench is a stocky man, a full head of gray hair, slumped down, with a walker beside him. I extend my hand, leaning down to try and catch his eye, since he barely lifts his head. "Hi, you must be Brian. I'm Beth. Can you tell me a bit about what is going on?"

He recaps the part about the failed hip replacement, tears streaming down his cheeks. Then he says, "I was a corpsman in the Navy. Now I'm an ICU nurse. I've raised a family. I'm the one everyone goes to for help. For God's sake, I used to jump out of helicopters into freezing cold water to rescue people. Now I can't do anything, I feel so worthless. I have to ask for help all the time. I couldn't even drive myself here. I don't know how I can go on like this if it doesn't get better."

I see students arriving, so I cut to the chase. "Brian, this evening we're going to start class with a meditation called the body scan. All you have to do is lie down or sit, and listen. You don't have to say anything to anyone if you don't want to. Afterward I'm going to give you some material to take home. Okay?" He nods and we walk in together.

I see people greeting each other, and can't help but note that Zach is there. (Yay! Okay, so I am attached to the guy, I confess.)

I settle into my seat, saying hello as I do so. Next to me is Joe, a slim older man I didn't really connect with last week. He leans toward me: "I couldn't hear a damned thing you said last week, and these chairs, my God, how the hell do you expect anyone to reduce their stress in these things?" He growls and yanks the chair back angrily.

I'm noticing that the stress reduction teacher—me—is feeling stressed and cranky all of a sudden. I'm having some mildly unkind thoughts, and I feel somewhat defensive too. *Okay, Beth, breathe.*

"I'm glad you're sitting closer to me, Joe," I say, "and I'll try to speak up. I can save this seat next to me for you in the future." I see he has brought a special cushion. "I hope that helps. If it doesn't, let me know."

I think he might be disappointed he didn't get the fight he was looking for. I remember now he's had numerous back surgeries and is in a lot of pain. He is seventy-seven years old and has been living with pain for a long time. He told us the last surgery was the last one he can have. I give him credit for trying this program at this time in his life.

It's also a time for me to practice what I am teaching, as I notice my own reactivity to Joe's comment. I pause and feel my breath and remember that he is here because he is suffering.

Class 2 begins with the body scan meditation. It is an opportunity for us to practice together, seeing how it is now, after a week of home practice. The body scan meditation is highlighted early in our series of classes to continue building awareness of body sensations, which will help us as we move forward in exploring stress as it manifests in the body. The body scan has many functions, including to aid healing because, to quote Jon Kabat-Zinn, "It's easier to heal a body that you are actually in."

I direct everyone to get into their preferred body scan position. As usual in week two, people are prepared with a few more props, such as blankets and pillows. I've got my eye on Brian, who is staying seated.

We finish the practice and I invite people to get into groups of three. Then I say, "So in a moment I'm going to ask you to share about this body scan. The one we just did. Not the one you did last Tuesday, or the meditation you learned in the seventies." I've learned to say this through eavesdropping: sometimes I overhear them talking about their pets or even a good restaurant. "And we're going to share in a particular way, that is, what did you experience during this body scan? It's not so much an evaluation, as in it was good or bad, or I did poorly or well, or the teacher was bad. Not like a movie review: loved him, hated her...Rather, see if you can capture and share with each other what actually happened. For example, 'I couldn't feel my toes, but my calves felt kind of achy; during the arms I was thinking about my daughter and then I think I fell asleep.' " I give these instructions because sharing in this way is a mindfulness practice in itself. It fosters a way of speaking and listening that is different from our habitual patterns and keeps folks close to their experience, which *is* practice!

I make sure everyone is partnering up as I go over to Brian and ask if he wants to join a group, or would prefer to share with me. "I'll share with you," he whispers. We sit close together. I lean toward his side and I can still see the rest of the room. He looks quite changed. "I didn't think I could do it, and I am almost afraid to say it, but I was able to concentrate, and for the first time in ages I stopped thinking about my problems. At first it seemed impossible, but I did it." I have a hunch some of his military training is kicking in for him now.

"So you were able to follow along and..."

"Well, I just felt my body and listened to your voice. It's very soothing." A small smile. "I want to keep doing it."

"Well, I have some good news for you, this is your homework, and I have a CD for you with the body scan on it. Now keep in mind that it may not always be like that, but just continue trying it and we'll see what happens. Is it okay if I introduce you to the group? Everyone got a chance to say why they are here last week and I just want them to know you're here. You can say as much or as little as you want." He nods.

I invite everyone to recreate our large circle, and introduce Brian. He quickly tells his story with a few tears, but fewer than earlier. Then I ask the group to share. "How was that for you? And it's okay to talk about your whole week of body scans now, or mindful eating—anything you were aware of, including not practicing."

"It's really changing the way I am with my pain. When I really feel my body, it's like I told you last week, and it's not how I think it is. In fact, I'm starting to question other things that I believe," says Jean, who's looking bright this evening.

"Not me," says Eileen, a sixth-grade teacher who said she mainly came because of work stress. "I am so much more aware of the pain in my neck, and my right shoulder is killing me.

Can you explain why I should do this when it seems to hurt more?"

This is a common question, and I'm glad it has come up. "Well, first of all, I hear you," I reply. "It really can make the pain more vivid in a way, and I can certainly see why you'd have that question." People look interested. "What do you think? Why might it be worthwhile to do even though it feels more uncomfortable right now?"

She pauses. "Maybe I need to know about it so I can do something about it?"

"That's possible. Given that it was so uncomfortable, what kept you from jumping up and running out of the room? How did you work with it?"

Another pause. Often people aren't aware that they already met a challenge with courage. "I felt it and then I'd listen to your voice and feel some other part. But I kept coming back to the pain in my neck."

"It sounds like there was quite a lot of awareness of your whole experience, especially given the challenge."

She looks surprised and then pleased for a moment.

A young physician named Nikki pipes up: "I found I was really impatient, I mean halfway through the first leg I started dreading the second leg, thinking, geez, I don't think I can get through a whole other leg, this is taking so long! Can we just get on with it? I have so much to do!"

"Is that feeling familiar to you? Do you ever feel that way about anything else?"

She thinks for a moment and then laughs. "Only everything!" Everyone laughs. Even Joe.

We hear the full range of reports: the good, the bad, and the in-between. For many people it is a new experience to feel their bodies just as they are, without trying to change or manipulate anything. In my medical practice I see so many diseases and conditions that come from the neglect of the signals of the body. I often feel that people are much more connected to their cars—and take better care of them, for that matter. Not to mention their cats or dogs! I get the feeling that if they could, they would simply drop their body off with me and say, "Hey, Beth, can you just tune this thing up for me? It makes a funny clunking sound and isn't running very smoothly." Whenever I share this with a group I can see it strikes a chord.

I sometimes tell them about a patient of mine, a nurse with a frozen shoulder. That's a shoulder that doesn't have much range of motion. Because of some tendonitis, it hurts to move it and so the motion becomes more limited over time. Helen had a painful shoulder from lifting patients, and kept putting off doing anything about it for months. By the time she came to see me, she could barely move it at all. It takes a long time to recover from a frozen shoulder; it is painful, difficult, and time consuming. However, it's pretty easy to treat tendonitis if you catch it early. This answers the question that Eileen was asking earlier, about why we might bring awareness to discomfort.

Last week I had new patient, Will, a lovely guy, a building contractor, who came in following his newly diagnosed diabetes. He found out about his diabetes while in the hospital to have his foot amputated. He couldn't feel his feet because of the (unknown) diabetes and a nonhealing wound went unattended for way too long. In fairness to Will, he didn't neglect his body simply out of distractedness or disconnect. He has a strong sense of duty to his family and his business, and like so many people, he put them first, seeing this as a service. What we fail to see is that if we don't care for the vehicle through which we provide that service, no one benefits and we actually become a liability. I'm not being dramatic, dear readers; it's just a good idea to maybe, you know, feel your body. Inhabit it, even if it feels worse in the beginning. It's the only one you've got and you won't be able to trade it in.

This is precisely what happened to the Buddha when he practiced asceticism, starving the body. He almost died doing it. But denial of the body, as the Buddha and many others have discovered, isn't the path to peace. To awaken means to be aware of our experience moment to moment—what's going on inside and outside.

The Second Noble Truth: There Is a Cause of Suffering

Sometimes the Buddha is described as the consummate physician because he saw the illness, suffering (the First Noble Truth), he made the diagnosis, the cause of suffering (the Second Noble Truth), described the cure, the possibility of the end of suffering (the Third Noble Truth) and gave the prescription, the Eightfold Path (the Fourth Noble Truth). We will explore all of these in subsequent chapters.

When the Buddha said there was a cause of suffering, he didn't simply mean old age, sickness, and death, he meant the way we relate to the challenging realities of life. The word he used to describe the cause of suffering in Pali is *tanha*, which is often translated as "unquenchable thirst." *Tanha* is also translated as "craving," with its counterpart being "aversion." By looking deeply into his own experience, the Buddha saw that we suffer because we want things to be different than they are (aversion), or we want to cling to what we have or used to have or we wish that something pleasant would stay the same (craving). The power of "craving" to cause suffering is the Second Noble Truth. It's important to make the distinction that when he said suffering, he didn't mean only the great tragedies and crises of our lives, but the more subtle sense of things not being quite right, not quite the way we wish they were. I don't know about you, but I have never been able to get my life to line up just so and then stay that way. Accepting that life isn't the way we want it to be can be very challenging, and we can create this ongoing sense of dissatisfaction.

Take Brian, for instance. He has indeed a very tough situation. His hip replacement failed. But his suffering is in part because he is having difficulty accepting that. He is caught in repetitive, if understandable, thoughts about how "it shouldn't have gone that way, it wasn't supposed to go that way, the usual recovery time is five weeks, and I should be back to work by now." He is caught in his thoughts—his aversion toward the way things are and his craving for things to be different, which in turn create powerful emotions. When he put the thoughts down for even a few minutes and simply felt his body in the moment, his suffering was greatly reduced. Joe, too, is suffering from physical pain with an anatomical cause, but he is also suffering from everything that he perceives is not right—in the room, with me, with the chair. That is where his mind goes. And even Nikki, with her good sense of humor, has some craving to get on to the next thing, and aversion to being still.

This is not to say that the experiences each of these people are having aren't genuinely difficult. They are. But what is happening with Brian and Joe and Nikki becomes more difficult because of the mind's tendency to "crave" or resist.

How We Handle Pain

There is a clear and helpful teaching from the Buddha on this phenomenon, which he called "the second arrow." The Buddha once asked a student, "If you were struck by an arrow, would it hurt?" The student answered, "It would." The Buddha then asked, "If you were struck by a second arrow, would that be even more painful?" The student answered, "Yes!" The Buddha then said, "In life, we usually can't control the first arrow. We can see the second arrow as our reaction to the first. We can see the second arrow as optional."

For example, you may recall in chapter 1 that Jean realized her thoughts about her pain were different and much worse than her actual experience of the sensation that she labels pain. Brian's thoughts and feelings about his plight, including how things were before the surgery and his fear of what may or may not happen in the future, are the second arrow. So are Joe's responses to the room, the chair, and me. You might take a moment here to consider an example where there is a first and second arrow in your own life.

My Zen teacher Tenshin Roshi often asks us, "If you were struck by an arrow, would you start by wondering who shot it? Why they shot it? Where it was made? Did you deserve it?" His questions prompt me to see that the wise thing to do would be to start by removing the arrow and taking care of the wound. In order to do that, we will have to look at the wound, feel it, and perhaps ask for help. For example, someone says something that feels hurtful. I could go into analyzing why she said it, or what I may have done to deserve it. I could in fact make up quite an elaborate story about it, complete with evidence, signed affidavits, and photos of her "wrongness." I call this making my case. Or I could simply attend to the fact that I feel hurt and take care of myself, or speak with a wise person (in other words, someone who won't add gasoline to the fire) and see what is actually true right now, before I address what happened. In my experience, if I do this first, I don't have to build a case. I've acknowledged my feelings and don't need a jury to acquit me or the other person, and I can then see the whole thing more clearly. When I do this, I can then perhaps realize that I do need more information, or perhaps I may let it go, or perhaps I need to address it. Meanwhile I haven't made things worse with a quick reaction or justification, in other words, a "second arrow."

What this means for us is twofold in the context of MBSR. First, we become aware of the thoughts that create the second arrow, and, using meditations like the body scan, we practice simply becoming aware of our direct experience without the stories (for example, the thought that this sensation is "killing me" is not the sensation itself). Second, by coming into the body more directly, experiencing what is happening without our habitual stories, we create an anchor of mindfulness for ourselves in our bodies. What is meant by direct experience? The thought or picture of an apple is not the sensory experience of biting into one. Experiencing the body in this way, according to the Buddha's teachings, is one of the best places we can be to begin to break the hold craving and aversion have on our minds. To do this, we have to do something that is very radical in our Western worldview: we must turn toward our experience rather than trying to deny it, avoid it, or escape it. Please don't take my word for it, or the Buddha's for that matter. Try and see if it is true for you.

Attending with Awareness

Everything we've just discussed above—observing the first and second arrow, and the cause of suffering—requires that we use some nonjudgmental, present-moment awareness of our experience. This is the foundational practice of mindfulness. The Pali word for mindfulness is *sati*. *Sati* appears many places throughout the Buddha's teachings. What does *sati* mean? Some scholars have said that it includes a sense of remembering or recollection, not as in remembering an event or story, but in the sense of coming home to a way of being we may not have felt for a long time. Many students in MBSR report this feeling after just a short time of practice. They might say, "I was simply present when the clouds passed overhead, I don't remember seeing them quite that way since I was a child." This is much like the experience the Buddha had, which I described in the Introduction, when he recalled a natural contentment arising as he simply sat under a tree and watched a festival. I like this idea of re-collecting, collecting parts of us that may have become disconnected, as in body and mind or mind and heart. Others scholars have said that *sati* means "present-moment awareness," and others "to stand by or near."

For the purposes of our exploration of mindfulness in the context of this book, let's work with MBSR founder Jon Kabat-Zinn's definition: mindfulness is "the awareness that arises when we pay attention on purpose in the present moment, nonjudgmentally." Also helpful is that of Buddhist teacher Christina Feldman, who says, "Mindfulness is the willingness and capacity to be equally near all events and experiences with kindness, curiosity, and discernment." One striking thing to me about both of these definitions is the fact that they involve our participation. We're invited to be "on purpose" and have some degree of willingness, and to expand our capacity. We've already seen this in our participants, and perhaps you've experienced this as well. As both Kabat-Zinn and Feldman imply, when we cultivate mindfulness we are able to touch our experiences, even the most painful ones, with kindness and openness rather than aversion and craving.

Of the various ways to translate the word *sati*, I particularly like: "To stand by or near; to attend with awareness." I experience a feeling of friendship when I contemplate this and when I practice mindfulness. Someone is standing near, kindly curious and attentive to my experience, and it is me.

The Four Foundations of Mindfulness

In his thorough examination of this human life, the Buddha found four areas or fields where we may establish mindfulness, and through these practices, experience freedom. They are called the Four Foundations of Mindfulness and are written about in a text called the *Satipatthana Sutta*, also referred to as the *Discourse on the Four Foundations of Mindfulness*. Please see the list of Recommended Readings in the back of this book for a beautiful, clear translation of this Sutta or Discourse by

Buddhist monk and scholar Anâlayo. Here the Buddha gave detailed practice instructions: a "how-to" manual, if you will. It is not a conceptual or theoretical teaching. He described these practices as the "direct path for the surmounting of sorrow, for the disappearance of discontent, for acquiring the true method for the realization of peace..." I don't know about you, but with this endorsement he's got my attention. Let's take a look at the first one, shall we?

The First Foundation of Mindfulness: Mindfulness of the Body

The First Foundation of Mindfulness, said the Buddha, is awareness of the body, starting by placing awareness on the breath. This is a fundamental practice in MBSR and in many Buddhist and other wisdom practices. He doesn't tell us how to breathe, but rather suggests that we "know a long breath to be long and a short breath to be short, we know an in breath and we know an out breath." In other words, he invites us to simply be aware of our breath as it is naturally. In MBSR we give instructions like: "Feel the breath" or "Be aware of the sensations of a breath, the rising and falling of the chest and belly." We don't actually teach people how to breathe. What's funny is that when you ask people what was most useful in the class, they often respond: "The breathing." And I want to ask in that moment, "What breathing? The one you've been doing all your life?" What they really mean is they found refuge in simply directing their attention to what is already and always happening. This is in part, I think, why the Buddha emphasized breathing practice so strongly. Many folks, myself included, have found this practice to be a direct path to freedom, if only for a moment. Try it and see what happens for you. You can also access an audio for this meditation at www.newharbinger. com/39164 (Track 3: Brief Breath Awareness).

The instructions on the First Foundation of Mindfulness in and of the body go on to invite awareness of postures—sitting, standing, walking, and lying down—as well as a reflection on what the body is made up of: fluids, bones, organs, hair, nails, teeth, flesh, sinews, and so on. The comprehensive list includes thirty-two components in all. The Buddha doesn't ask us to judge the body or change the body, but to place our mindfulness there, which allows us to get to know it and attend to it. We've heard some reasons to attend to it more readily, but this seeing it somewhat impersonally as made up of components—which everyone has—might help us be less judgmental and even more connected to the rest of humanity. I had a lovely young woman student who struggled a lot with body image. She was constantly thinking about her weight and her appearance; it was a source of great suffering for her and nothing she had tried before could break the grip of these thoughts. After trying the body scan and mindful walking, she reported, "I wasn't fat, I wasn't thin, I wasn't too anything. I was just me standing. Suddenly I felt so much gratitude for my feet and my legs, I felt so grateful for this body. And then I realized that everyone has one—a body, I mean—and it may sound strange, but I felt less alone. I don't know if I have ever felt this way before." Tears streamed down her face, and a profound transformation had begun simply by bringing mindfulness into the body.

In the culture of the Buddha's time, the body was seen as something to transcend, and even to revile. This is common in other spiritual traditions as well. In the culture of our time, the attitude to the body is often one of disconnect. And even more than disconnection, when we think about our body, we are usually evaluating it, measuring it, and wanting to change or manipulate it as if it were more of an object than a living, experiential, functioning gift. (Have you thought about your amazing thyroid or kidneys lately? How about the cells of your pancreas or your brain?)

I ask you, how do you relate to your body? Do you see it in slightly imperfect parts? As in "I hate my thighs." (Poor thighs, they didn't do anything). We may apply makeup to it, change our hair color, and have things operated on, put it on severely restricted diets, exercise it—not for the joy of movement and health, but to actually punish it for eating. Certainly we criticize it. But what if the body was a source of wisdom, calm, and joy? What about that as a possibility?

Bodily Experience as Teacher on Impermanence

In the teaching on the First Foundation of Mindfulness—Mindfulness of the Body—and throughout the entire *Discourse on the Four Foundations of Mindfulness* (*Satipatthana Sutta*) there is a refrain that is repeated thirteen times. Part of the refrain invites us to contemplate "the nature of arising in the body and passing away in the body." In other words, to stay present and pay attention on purpose long enough to see that things change, including things we were sure were constant.

When Jean practiced the body scan for the first time, she became aware that sensations are not constant, that they do indeed "arise and pass away," quite differently than her original description of her pain, which was, "My body hurts all over, all the time." This realization alone reduced some of her suffering. Notice how it feels if you use terms like "I always feel like this." And now, "Sometimes I feel like this, and sometimes like that..." This points to another essential teaching of the Buddha, ever the keen observer: the teaching on impermanence. He really wanted us to see this phenomenon—the ever-present nature of change. When we get more aware of, and comfortable with, the changing nature of reality, we suffer less. We'll continue to explore the important Buddhist teaching on impermanence as we go forward.

The other handy thing about practicing mindfulness of the body and the breath is that they are always with us. With practice, we can choose to direct our attention to the sensations of the body and interrupt a painful thought-emotion cycle. No equipment is required, or any special postures, or even silence. It translates very well into daily life. For example, if I am having a difficult patient encounter and find myself getting aggravated or scared (which I know because I feel it in my body), I can quickly and quietly direct my attention to the soles of my feet or my bottom on the seat of my rolling stool, or simply feel the rise and fall of my belly with a breath or two. This prevents me from escalating the emotion and allows me to maintain some clarity and stability when I need it the most.

In practicing a meditation dedicated to feeling the body with mindfulness in a nonjudgmental and noninterfering way, we see many things. For one thing, we take it less personally, we realize it doesn't define us, and yet paradoxically we own it more, which means we care for it more. And awareness of our body allows us to listen to the wisdom of the body's signals. I often elicit from students the language we already have about such wisdom. We say, for example, "I had a gut feeling about it," or "My heart wasn't in it," or "I was so mad I couldn't see straight!" Have you ever had the thought or awareness that something just didn't *feel* right? What happened when you didn't pay attention to that? What happens when you do? For me, when I ignore these promptings I often find myself wishing I hadn't, and when I pay attention to them, I often see the wisdom that is there.

Lastly, for now, remember the raisin exercise? Or any experience of mindful eating or mindfulness of daily activities? Many folks share that they had no idea how pleasurable it could be to eat one or two raisins. Often the nurses I work with say that mindful hand washing has added many small moments of pleasure and relaxation to their busy day. So awareness of the body may also inform our capacity for the simple joy of being alive, through the powerful doorways of our senses. See if this is true for you. I can't tell you how often the feeling of the breeze on my face or the sound of a blue jay has awakened me out of a worried thought stream and brought me back to peace of the moment.

At the end of class I encourage the students to continue with the body scan every day, and to find in their workbooks a page called the "Pleasant Events Calendar." "You'll see in your workbook a daily log to record pleasant events," I say. "It asks you certain questions like, What did the event feel like in terms of sensations? What were the thoughts associated with it? And what were the emotions? I invite you to approach it like this: You're an anthropologist visiting the culture of Nikki or Zach or Raúl. What do Raúls find pleasant? What components make it what Carols call pleasant? It's different for everyone. Try being genuinely curious and scientific about it. It doesn't have to be something big, with fireworks and a brass band. On the other hand, it also doesn't have to read: 'Monday: Beautiful sunset. Tuesday: Beautiful sunset...' There is a reason scientists are so intrigued by this practice: it is a similar mindset brought to an experiment or research of any kind. What is considered pleasant in the culture of you and what makes it so?"

Brian is standing by the door with his walker. I see Louise waiting anxiously outside. I can almost read her thoughts: "Did it work?"

"Thank you, Beth." Brian says, as I hand him his materials.

"You're welcome. My phone number is on there. You can call me any time."

Zach stops by. "Hey, Beth, see ya later." He reaches out his hand. I take it.

Norma and Alan, the couple dealing with pancreatic cancer, linger. I move toward them. "We're doing the body scan twice a day; it's helping with the anxiety. Can we do it more than that?"

"Of course," I reply. "Also, last week I spoke about mindfulness of ordinary daily activities, like washing the dishes, showering, driving. What do you think about trying that?"

"I love to cook," Norma says, "but it's been difficult. Maybe I'll try practicing there."

Then I leave with a full and somewhat soggy heart, moved by the sincere question of this couple facing life and death with courage: that willingness to stand near their experience, their lives, just as they are right now.

Chapter 3

THE DHARMA OF CURIOSITY:
What Is Here Right Now?

Suddenly it's Thursday afternoon again and I am packing up to transition from the medical office to the MBSR classroom. Today I saw Lynn, who is one of the patients I referred to my MBSR class last year. Like many people from cold climates, Lynn came to Palm Desert shortly after retiring from her high-powered corporate position in Chicago. The first time I saw her, her blood pressure was so high it gave *me* high blood pressure. She'd already had one stroke. She struck me as someone who had had about five cups of strong coffee and four cigarettes before she came in, which after some careful history taking, turned out was quite accurate.

During the first six months of seeing her, I focused primarily on her blood pressure, afraid that she would have a more serious, catastrophic stroke. By the time I brought up MBSR, Lynn was on six antihypertensive medications and her blood pressure was still not under control. She had not had an easy retirement. She'd been a whistle blower regarding discrimination in the company she worked for and ended up in an expensive, protracted lawsuit that had not ended well. In fact it was still not resolved. Her wife, tired of the legal battles, had left her in the midst of this. Lynn was filled with grief, anger, and resentment.

During the class, she did meditation and yoga for the first time and found she really enjoyed them. She also liked being in the group, not having realized how lonely she was. She made friends with a young man in the class named Matt who was very shy, and they started to have adventures together.

Today's visit was a bit of a landmark. First of all, her blood pressure was almost within a normal-ish range. She still smoked, but much less, and the coffee was down too. But that's not what she was excited about.

"Beth, you're not going to believe what I have been doing."

"Tell me."

"Well, you know all those boxes from the lawsuit? I think there were about 27 of them, they took up a whole room in my condo."

"Yes."

"I got rid of all of them. I hired a shredding company and I'm letting it go."

"Wow."

"When I met you, that lawsuit consumed me. It was all I thought about—well, until Ronnie left. Then I had two things that dominated me. I remember distinctly in the first few weeks of the class when I began to get some breaks in my thoughts and started having little moments of, if not quite joy, I'd say I had some peace. And I began to open up to other people."

"I remember that, too. And you really connected with your classmates."

"Well, that has continued! Matt and I have been going to chanting at Urban Yoga, and the other day we went to Opera in the Park and had a picnic."

"I am so glad to hear it." Actually I was astounded. Seven years of litigation and she was now able to let it go. And have some fun in the bargain.

"That program of yours, it's really something. You know, I still do that body scan every day."

"Well, that's the thing, Lynn, it's not my program, it's yours. You did it, you *are* doing it."

"I've changed in ways I didn't even know were possible. I thought I was always going to feel the same way about the lawsuit and my breakup. It's remarkable to see the changes."

Yes it is, I think, and yet also not remarkable either. These *are* the fruits of regular practice in my experience, and another way impermanence shows up!

Lynn has been a great teacher for me. I had a very narrow agenda for her. I wanted her blood pressure to come down so her head wouldn't explode or worse. I wanted…See how that is? What on earth does what I want have to do with her life? She is living her life in a new way, and she is driving the boat.

Lynn's story and the changes she has experienced really bring to life what we'll be exploring in this chapter, what Jon Kabat-Zinn calls "glimpses of wholeness" in *Full Catastrophe Living*. People come to class with a sense of feeling contracted around their suffering, with self-referential thoughts about what happened to them or their diagnosis. Our idea of who we are becomes very small and life, too, becomes small. Then, simply by practicing and nurturing awareness, there begins to be some space where something new can happen.

In this chapter we'll see in the class, and in the Buddha's teaching, the way bringing curiosity through our practice may begin to create some spaciousness in our perceptions of our lives, and in our moment-to-moment experience as well. I invite you to pay attention to this as you read the stories and teachings. You could do it as a mindfulness practice!

I remember vividly one of my first glimpses of wholeness. At a very difficult time in my life, when I was in a lot of pain about my family, a young friend encouraged me to read a book by Zen master Thich Nhat Hanh, called *Peace Is Every Step*. It was my first introduction to the practice of mindfulness. He suggested that we simply give our full attention to whatever we were doing in the present moment, and he gave very specific examples, such as washing dishes and walking. This sounded more doable for me than meditation. So the next time I made dinner, I gave chopping carrots my full attention, seeing the bright color, smelling the fresh, sweet fragrance, feeling the weight and coolness of the knife in my hand. And for a few moments I was free.

We've talked about the First Noble Truth—suffering or *dukkha*—and the Second Noble Truth: the cause of suffering, craving for things to be other than the way they are (where Lynn was stuck for a long time). Later in the chapter we'll explore the Third Noble Truth, in which the Buddha teaches what Lynn experienced, and what I did for that brief carrot-cutting moment—that there is an end to suffering that is available to everyone. Maybe we can't experience it all the time as the Buddha did, but we do get greater and greater experiences of wholeness and freedom as time goes by and practice is sustained. And that, my friends, is the possibility of the end to suffering.

Mindfulness in Motion—Class 3

It's time for class. I've taken a short walk and eaten my dinner, letting go of the earlier part of my day. I see people entering the classroom, removing their shoes, and greeting each other. There is a feeling of warmth and friendliness. We are becoming a community, and a refuge—remember the Three Refuges? It's not unusual to see the third refuge of Sangha or community becoming stronger by class 3.

This evening we offer yet another doorway to the present moment and mindfulness by beginning with a long period of yoga on the floor. After our short "arriving meditation," I talk about the mindful movement. "This evening we're going to do a longer movement practice based in yoga. It's mostly done on the floor, but all of it can be adapted to a chair and I'll show how that is done. *Yoga* is an ancient word that actually means to yoke or unify. What do you think that means to us? What we are we yoking together?"

"The mind and the body?" Debbie answers.

"Yes, and maybe the heart too," I say, without going into the idea that in the West we believe these things are separate. "I want to talk a little bit about how we are going to approach this in the context of MBSR. There is an invitation here to bring the same curiosity and nonjudgmental awareness to the sensations of the movements themselves as we do in the body scan and with eating the raisin. The focus is not so much on getting to any particular pose or outcome, but to be curious about the whole process, including our friend, the mind—which sometimes does not seem so friendly. As we begin to practice, you may note that there may be some critical commentary up in your mental media box, like at a sporting event, evaluating your performance: 'Hey she's really stiff!' 'Oh, he's not performing like he did last season.' Are you familiar with that voice?" I see smiles and nods. "Do you think it's helpful?"

"Probably not, but that guy is always commenting on me. He's a bit of a downer," says Zach.

"So simply be aware that this may occur and, when you can—and I'll remind you—bring your attention back kindly and with consciousness to the sensations of the body as it moves, just as you have been doing in the body scan. When I ask you to check in with yourself and take care of yourself, not going beyond what feels right to you in the moment, this is a process you have been practicing daily for the last few weeks. You already know something about this type of caring attention."

And so we begin the mindful movement practice, with occasional cues to notice what the mind is up to and to feel the body from within and without. This is experiencing the First Foundation of Mindfulness I wrote about in chapter 2 in real time—noticing that there is a body and also the constantly changing nature of things. I move from floor to chair, while guiding, sitting close to Joe and Brian, and also to another woman, Francine, so they can see the adaptations. We do them together: "No one left out" is my intention.

After the final resting pose, gradually we come to sitting and I ask them to get into groups of three. "We're going to share with each other how this practice went, seeing if you can describe the actual experience rather than your version of the 'half-time' comments." I enjoy seeing them connecting with each other. The conversation is lively. I look forward to hearing what they have to say.

When we come back to the whole group, Peter, a business-man who said he was here because of "work stress," jumps in. "I never thought I could do yoga, I mean I thought it was all about getting your legs behind your head or something. I really enjoyed this and I was kind of surprised I could do it. I was nervous because I have a bad disc in my back. I think this might help. I really do not want surgery."

"How do you feel right now?"

"Alive. Tingly."

"I've been doing yoga for a long time," says Cindy, "so in some ways it was really easy physically, but it was so different without the judgment. I'm so used to pushing myself. This was more pleasurable. I saw how hard I am on myself. I'm looking forward to seeing if I can try this in my regular yoga practice." She told us in the first week that, despite her meditation and yoga practice, she has a pretty short fuse with her family, so I ask a question: "Any other areas of life where you think that approach might be interesting? I believe you said in the first week you wanted to take your practice more 'off the mat.'"

She smiles. "Oh yeah, I see what you are saying. I'll think about that. Is this going to be part of the home practice?"

"It is. We'll be alternating with the body scan, or you may do both."

"Thank God! I'd much rather move than lie still. I really prefer the yoga." I see a few heads nodding.

This is an interesting moment in the program, where people start expressing preferences and have some choices. I think of a classic Zen teaching attributed to the Third Zen Ancestor. The translation I studied begins like this: "The Great Way is not difficult for those who have no preferences." My Zen teacher Tenshin Roshi explained it like this: "It's not that we don't have preferences. Of course we do. But how do we handle it when we don't get them? Or when we do and then they end?" He is pointing here to the Second Noble Truth— the cause of suffering: the craving for things to be other than they actually are. Of course I don't say it in this way in the class. What I do say is: "It's fine to know what you prefer. But it's also good to ask, Where might I grow? What will stretch me into new territories to explore what I may have signed up to discover in this MBSR program in the first place? Often it's the practice you *don't* prefer. But I invite you to investigate this for yourself."

"The main thing," Tenshin Roshi said, "is to not prefer another life to the one you have." From time to time a teacher will say something that drops deeply inside and then ripples out in ever-widening circles for a long time. This statement for me was one of those teachings. I began to check in with myself more frequently and ask, Am I living *my* life right now? The only one I have? Or am I wrestling with it—striving for an alternative reality that suits my preferences and leads nowhere? I have found this to be a compelling line of inquiry. See how it is for you, if it serves in any way, or not.

I've noticed that people often prefer the movement practices, as Cindy expressed, and have more difficulties with ones like the body scan that emphasize stillness. But over the years of my own practice and teaching, I can't emphasize the value in practicing stillness enough. In life there are things we can't just walk away from. Alan's pancreatic cancer is a good example. He and Norma can't move away from that. June's son's bipolar disorder can't be run away from. In a recent MBSR series, I had a firefighter who was a super athlete, always on the go, even off the job. Then he was in a bad car accident that stopped him in his tracks. Not being able to relieve his stress with exercise was excruciating for him. The body scan, as well as the sitting meditation we'll get to in chapter 5, were lifesavers according to him. I often wonder if the Buddha's great awakening came in part from his commitment not to move from his seat until he had seen and learned what he most wanted to understand: how to live with some peace and ease in the face of suffering.

Having a regular practice can provide us with alternative tools to use whenever our usual "go-to" options are not available to us. I've learned about the power of this from other folks like the firefighter who had previously used constant activity and exercise as their main way of coping with stress and emotion. When they can't do that, they have no idea what to do until they learn something about being still. There is a line from Jon Kabat-Zinn in the Bill Moyers PBS segment on MBSR about having a daily practice that I often quote: "You want to start weaving the parachute long before you need it."

For now I just gently suggest that everyone stick with the home practice the way it is laid out and be curious about whatever happens day to day. As is often said in this part of the program, "For now you don't have to like it, just try it."

To return to our group dialogue, I continue: "So how did your week go? Any learnings from the Pleasant Events Calendar or any other practices?"

Renée's hand shoots up. "I was preparing one of my favorite meals. I really enjoy cooking it, not just eating it, and talking to my sister, which I also love to do. I don't usually do both at the same time. I found out I didn't actually enjoy either one as much as if I was doing one thing at time. If we weren't doing the Calendar I don't think I would have noticed that. It was actually a bit tiring. And with caring for my husband, I really need these pleasant moments."

"I noticed I have more pleasant moments than I thought I was having," says Zach.

"Would you be willing to share an example?"

"Oh sure, just ordinary stuff. Like taking a shower after the gym or petting our dog, Max."

"I felt like I had a hard time finding many pleasant moments," says Elaine. "But I wasn't really focusing on things like that. I just feel so overwhelmed in my day."

Norma raises her hand. "After we got Alan's diagnosis, I was so frightened I couldn't think. I was in shock. Now we do the body scan together twice a day, and I'm starting to calm down. We have some important decisions to make and I am just beginning to feel like I can face them. I guess I'd say the body scan is my pleasant event."

Brian says, "I'm not crying all the time. So that's a major improvement." He smiles and even chuckles a little. "I also found out my family likes being there for me. My daughter says she never had the chance before and she wants to help. Oh, shoot, I'm going to cry. Anyway, she says it's a way of showing me how much she loves me." He blows his nose and continues. "I'm scheduled for another surgery, so I may miss a class or two."

After we have done a short awareness of breath meditation, I give instructions for the week to come: "As I mentioned earlier, we now will be practicing the body scan alternating with yoga. This week we have a different experiment. It's called the Unpleasant Events Calendar." I hear a soft groan. "I know, I know, but let's think for a moment why exploring this might be interesting."

Silence. Then: "I have plenty of unpleasant events," Joe says. "For one thing, my partner! I could fill it in right now—breakfast, lunch, and dinner."

Joe's response is typical. Sometimes I ask the students, "How many of you think you could fill this out ahead of time? 'Staff meeting Tuesday, in-laws Friday…'?" This often elicits a big laugh of recognition, and then I encourage them to see what is really true.

"Thanks, Joe, it's true. Our relationships can be a challenging place in our lives. Does anyone else feel that way, and think some of these might show up on this Calendar?" Lots of hands go up. "Any other thoughts about why we might do this?"

"Maybe we can find out what makes it unpleasant and do something about it?"

"Maybe," I say. "And what do you think might happen when you become curious about the questions asked in the Calendar—the thoughts, feelings, and sensations?"

"Well," says Jean, "I notice in the body scan, when something bothers me, I try to be curious about it and then it often changes. It seems like soon after I start to bring attention to it without being so upset about it, like I was before, it somehow shifts my whole experience."

"Thanks, Jean." The students are teaching "the Buddha's" wisdom, which is in fact their own wisdom, all the time.

The Third Noble Truth: There Is an End to Suffering

The moment the Buddha invited us to examine the cause of suffering for ourselves, to deeply see into the way craving and aversion function in our lives and the after-effects of being motivated by them, he opened the door into the possibility of freedom. The Pali word for this liberation is Nibbana. The literal translation is "blowing out" or "quenching." What is quenched, you ask? The fires of craving and aversion. How do we extinguish them? The Buddha laid out a path for us in the Fourth Noble Truth, which we will be traveling in future chapters. In the Third Noble Truth, we open ourselves up to the reality that liberation is possible, even if we are not sure how. That's where curiosity comes in.

Another word for *Nibbana* you may be more familiar with is the Sanskrit term *Nirvana*, which is a band, yes, but is also frequently thought of as a place where everything is wonderful. Or a blissful state such as is seen on the faces of people in a yoga magazine, perched on a rock in Hawaii, looking transcendent in a tricky balancing pose.

I prefer to think of *Nibbana/Nirvana* as a space rather than a place. It is the space Norma and Alan are giving themselves to process this terminal diagnosis and the dramatic changes in their lives, by doing the body scan twice a day. It's the glimpses of peace Brian is experiencing in the space between the painful thoughts about his condition. Lynn experienced this space when she decided to let go of the lawsuit and all the masses of paperwork that went with it. Suddenly she had new space, not just in her condo, but in her mind and heart. Space for joy and peace.

As with all the teachings, the key element in reducing suffering begins with seeing first that we do suffer, and then how we suffer. We do this "seeing" with mindfulness, the kind, curious, and nonjudgmental awareness that says, "Ah, look at that! I'm uncomfortable! I'm gripped by something, I feel it in my body, and I see my mind racing to strategize my way out of this or trying cling to it." Then—perhaps—a question arises: "Is there something I am doing to make this worse?" And in this inquiry lies the possibility of relief, the living in new and wider pastures.

The Second Foundation of Mindfulness— Mindfulness of Feeling Tones

In class 3 we're looking deeply into the way we experience the world through the Pleasant Events Calendar and the Unpleasant Events Calendar. This relates to the Second Foundation of Mindfulness, which is called Mindfulness of *Vedana*, or establishing awareness in the realm of feelings. You might immediately think: "Oh, I know this, 'feelings' equals emotions. Happy, sad, angry, lonely. I think I've pretty much covered that in therapy." But that's not exactly what's meant by the word *vedana*. The interesting thing about using the Pali words is that they stop the mind for a moment and cause us to say, "What the heck is that?" Because no matter how we try to translate them, we can only approximate what was meant, and that means exploring the unknown a little more.

Here's what is meant by *vedana*: feeling tones or sensations that are categorized as pleasant, unpleasant, and neutral. These occur almost immediately when our internal senses come in contact with external objects, and they come *before* what we in the West think of as feelings. You'll see how participants in MBSR classes investigate the way they label things and how that affects their actual lived experience. This is the practice of the Second Foundation of Mindfulness. Here we get to explore the way we quickly interpret the world and our experiences as soon as we come in contact with it. Is it pleasant, unpleasant, or neutral? The very question itself gives a wider perspective.

Here's essentially how the Buddha explained it in the *Discourse on the Four Foundations of Mindfulness*. He directs the monks to contemplate feeling tones in a particular way—with a "knowing" that is not intellectual but rather has qualities of curiosity, openness, and nonjudgment. He asks them, when feeling a pleasant feeling, to know: "I feel a pleasant feeling." When feeling an unpleasant feeling, to know: "I feel an unpleasant feeling." When feeling a neutral feeling, to know: "I feel a neutral feeling." The Buddha is not giving us any instruction to do anything, he is simply inviting us to know what we're feeling, to see the way we quickly categorize things, and then to see how that awareness may increase or decrease suffering.

In class this week we've just come back with information about our lives from the Pleasant Events Calendar home practice assignment. In order to do this, we have to bring some genuine curiosity to what we label as pleasant and then explore it further with the particular questions asked in the Calendar: "What sensations were present? What thoughts? What feelings?" (Here, by "feelings" we mean emotions.)

One benefit of this is to "know" what's happening when it's happening. To know in the way the Buddha means "know" is to have a broader and present-moment awareness of what is unfolding in our minds. This is more about nonjudgmental knowing than about the content. Another benefit is to begin to separate the feeling tone or sensation and recognize the label we are putting on it—good, bad, pleasant, unpleasant.

The intention of this exercise is in part to bring awareness to pleasant things we may miss, but also to practice this kind of investigation in all things. When a pleasant moment goes by unnoticed, then our lives are less enjoyable. However, when we get super excited about a pleasant event, what happens when it is over? In the summer MBSR class a student reported, "My family and I were really enjoying our carefully planned vacation at the beach." (Meanwhile, mind you, it's 115 degrees in the desert.) "Three days before it was over I found myself dreading the end—thinking about going back to work, juggling the kids' activities and the heat. I caught myself unable to enjoy the time we still had there. Then I remembered the practice of coming into the present moment, and it helped."

This is not to say we shouldn't get passionate about things, it's just helpful to know it so that it doesn't lead to the unconscious behavior of chasing more! Or to becoming clouded by anticipation of the end, as our student described here. When I set this up in week two, I try to be careful to emphasize the curiosity factor by using an anthropologist analogy: "Be an anthropologist of your own life. What is called 'pleasant' in the culture of you?"

Sometimes we may find that what we call pleasant, and do in a habitual way because the label has stuck, is actually not that pleasant. One student from the UK had just such a revelation: "I am a soccer fanatic and I arranged our whole Saturday so my family would end up in a pub where I could watch the match. I noticed a bunch of things. One, I was actually quite tense, knowing my wife would have to keep the kids entertained so I could do what I wanted to do. Two, my whole body was clenched most of the time in anxiety about who would score. And because my team wasn't doing that well, emotionally I was upset! Afterward I thought, 'What was so pleasant about that?' Before, I would have sworn that watching a soccer match was definitely pleasant."

On the other hand, like Zach, we may find that taking a shower is much more pleasant with awareness than when we are lost in thought. And we get to do it every day.

At the end of this class, I see clusters of people talking with each other, smiling, leaning toward each other as they speak. Zach lends Joe a hand while he puts on his shoes. Renée is talking animatedly with Nikki. I sit for a moment before I get up and soak in the collective warmth, the connectedness, and what really does feel like a true refuge. At least I know it surely is for me.

Chapter 4

THE DHARMA OF AWARENESS:
Turning Toward Stress

Today certainly had its challenges. My wonderful medical assistant Angela's ten-year-old son was sick. He was home with grandma, but she's not in such good shape either. I felt for Angela, aware of her divided attention. I told her to go home, and that I would check my own patients in—her son comes first. She, in her usual committed and loyal way, refused, but I could tell she appreciated the option.

I have to admit, work would be really hard without her. Our schedule is packed, and that's only the half of it. The doctor was not in yesterday, so there is an unusually high pile of charts with labs to be reviewed, specialists' consults to read, and piles and piles of prescriptions to be filled (or not). Then there are the phone messages.

The stress reduction teacher is somewhat stressed. It's challenging practicing medicine these days, learning a new electronic medical record system, checking lots of boxes for insurance billing purposes, and most of all, so much of many appointment visits are spent listening to the patients' unhappiness with the system. I try to be a good advocate, but sometimes all I can say is, "I'm as frustrated as you are."

Fortunately, I'm aware of it. Years ago, I would not even know I was stressed out. I would just ignore my own experience, leave myself at the door, and feel pretty burdened and dry at the end of the day. But through mindfulness practices, I became aware of this pattern and that it was not serving me or my patients. I became aware that self-neglect increases stress and leads to burnout. So I started a practice I call "I'm here too." I do this when I put on my white coat. As I put my arms in the sleeves I say to myself, "I'm in here." And I try to hold myself kindly while being there for other people. It makes a real difference.

As I drive to class this evening, I am not entirely alone. In the back seat is an old friend Hugh and I affectionately call "Stress Organ Guy." It's a great visual aid that Hugh created. He took a dry-erase whiteboard and in permanent inks drew the outline of a human, showing colorful organs affected by stress. We are quite fond of Stress Organ Guy. He comes with us on all kinds of adventures, to schools, nonprofit organizations, and county agencies like the child protective service agency where we taught last week. He's starting to be a bit worn around the edges, but he makes his point.

I tune in to my mind-body-heart and realize I need to center myself a bit more before I teach. So I take some time to slowly walk in the grass barefoot before I head to the classroom. Ah, much better.

People are settling in, it feels safe and peaceful in the MBSR classroom. And there is also a feeling of excitement, a kind of "I wonder what is going to happen next?" energy. I see people watching curiously as I put Stress Organ Guy on the easel.

This evening we'll start with some yoga, followed by walking meditation, and then a seated practice—awareness of breathing. We're building longer periods of meditation practices as we continue with the curriculum. We began with forty-five minutes in week one and are now at ninety minutes in week four. Perhaps as you read along and practice with us, you might see what it's like to add some more time to your personal practices.

I let everyone know that Brian has had his surgery and is doing well. Then I invite everyone to stand, but before they actually do it I suggest that they pay attention to how the body knows how to stand, what it feels like—the mechanics—as if they have never done it before. "Stand as if it is the most interesting new yoga pose you have ever tried." I wonder if I can actually feel Joe rolling his eyes. I see Renée smiling as she carefully stands.

I continue my instructions: "Now that we're standing, feeling the soles of your feet on the floor. As much surface area as you can feel."

(Incidentally, notice how in my instructions to the class I tend to use the gerund rather than the imperative—"*feeling* the soles of your feet" rather than "*feel* the soles of your feet." This is a basic practice of MBSR, aimed at avoiding the sense of authoritarian, "top down" teaching.)

As I stand, I think of how difficult it is for Brian to stand on his wobbly hip and for Joe with his degenerative spine.

We continue to the end of the yoga series, then I give the instructions for walking meditation: simply feeling the sensations of the feet and legs walking, moving much more slowly than usual. "And now when the mind wanders—which it will—bringing it back to the act of walking itself." I give them a few minutes to try it. Sometimes this is the perfect practice for me, like the walk I just did between patient care and this class. In the Zen tradition, walking meditation or *kinhin* is considered a transition practice because it is more similar to daily life than sitting. It gives us a chance to practice paying attention and moving at the same time. Then we go on from there to paying attention to—well, everything!

"And now, finding your seat," I say. "We're going to move into a seated meditation that is a little longer than we've done so far. I'll be giving some instructions around focusing on the breath. One thing to try out with this one is working with stillness of the body. So when you feel an itch, see what happens if you don't scratch it immediately." The problem with this instruction is that I myself always start to itch everywhere as I give it, and other people do too. But it's important! "Do it as an experiment, not like 'Oh, Beth says we shouldn't scratch, so I won't. She says not to move, so I won't.' " I demonstrate someone sitting rigidly. "It's not a blind rule; rather it's a place of exploration. What happens if I don't scratch? Believe it or not, it's pretty interesting. So we're taking a little trip into the unknown here. It's not just the body that wants to move, what else moves?"

"My mind!" says Zach. "It moves, and I mean a lot!" Lots of nods.

"Exactly! It does and it will—that's perfectly natural. So when you notice it, simply bring awareness back to the body, the breath. No criticism required. No beatings. And there is no 'attention-ometer' rating how many times your mind wanders. This is between you and you. Please know the same thing is going on for everyone. No matter how calm other people look, trust me, their mind is up to something! It's simply the nature of the mind. It wanders."

We begin this longer meditation, and from time to time I drop in reminders to feel the breath, not control it or think it, and to gently bring the mind back when it wanders. I'm struck by the stillness in the room. It feels like a deep pond on a quiet day with no wind. You can access an audio of this meditation at www.newharbinger.com/39164 (Track 4: Twenty-Minute Awareness of Breath Meditation).

After I ring the bell, I ask, "So...what did you notice?"

Norma says, "I was amazed how much time I spent worrying—was I doing it right? Will Alan be okay? Will I be okay? But I could come back when you reminded us."

Alan says, "My mind is really busy, it seemed like I was just thinking about our plans, and upcoming appointments, test results, and so on most of the time."

"So you noticed thinking going on. Then what happened? What did you do?"

"I heard your voice; it felt like you were reading my mind…"

"Right!" chimes in Zach.

"And then I came back to the breath."

"You just described meditation," I respond.

"I wondered about that," says Jean, "after trying meditation so many times over the years and being frustrated, this time I just thought, maybe coming back *is* meditation!"

"So is it?" I ask.

"I think so. It's the not judging myself that is so different."

"I think you may be on to something," I remark. "Any other experiences?"

"I tried not scratching an itch," says Peter. "It was strange, but it actually went away and I forgot about it until just now."

"My knees really hurt all day," says Carol. "But for some strange reason they are not bothering me now. I mean, they hurt, but it doesn't bother me in the same way. Not sure how to explain it. And I didn't do anything."

Peter and Carol are both demonstrating the value of sitting with a sensation and not interfering with it. They get to see the "arising and passing away," the impermanence of the sensations, and in Carol's case her emotions about the sensation too, *and* they are also slowing down the process of automatic habitual reactivity—itch-scratch, knee pain-move… This space between sensation and reaction starts in meditation and then translates over time to more complex situations in our lives. This is one of many powerful benefits of sitting meditation. See what you find in your own practice!

"The way you keep reminding us to come back without judgment, gently and kindly—I find that is rippling out to other areas in my life. I am a little less hard on myself sometimes." Nikki smiles after she speaks.

I thank everyone, and ask about the last week's practice, especially the Unpleasant Events Calendar.

Eileen leans forward in her chair and says, "I received a note asking me to come to the principal's office." People laugh;

everyone knows that feeling. "Yeah, but she's my boss!" she continues. "Anyway, on the way there I felt my heart racing and my mouth got dry. I wondered if it was about losing my temper last week with Billy, a child who drives me nuts. Maybe his parents complained. I started mustering my defense about our ridiculous work load and why it's not my fault. And all of the sudden I thought about that stupid Calendar. I didn't really think about it so much as go: "This is an unpleasant event and it hasn't even happened yet!" More laughter.

"And?" I prompt.

"She just wanted to tell me that someone from another school is coming to visit, and she would like to show them the history circle I created. I have this certain way of teaching history."

"So it wasn't exactly what you thought."

"No, and then I started to wonder how often I do that—have stressful moments before they happen, and maybe I don't even notice that it turned out differently. I also realized I still feel really badly about that interaction with Billy and I need to address it."

Then Joe spoke up. "I've been having this major problem in a relationship. I've been so frustrated that I can't get my partner to do what I want him to do. He doesn't understand me. But this week something changed."

"Oh?"

"Yeah, Joe's on to Joe." He taps his temple with a sly grin.

"Can you say more about that?" I ask.

"Well, we were starting into one of our usual arguments and then I noticed that my body felt very tense. I was so irritated, which is normal for me, but I saw it, I felt it, and I paused for a moment before I said anything. I asked myself, what really is the problem here? And I realized that at least part of it is simply the way I'm looking at it. I think it should be my way or the highway. But he sees it differently. A lot can happen in that pause, or rather not happen, like another damn argument. Yep, Joe's on to Joe."

In my first MBSR teacher training, Saki Santorelli, the Executive Director of the UMASS Center for Mindfulness, said, "You'll see that in no time the curriculum will come pouring out of the students." What more could I possibly add to what Joe and Eileen have seen and said? I love how the students teach the class, and teach me. They are constantly reminding me that we are all Buddhas; we all have the capacity to awaken.

Raúl, who has been mostly quiet so far, is being nudged by his wife. "My kids, they are coming up to me and hugging me more, just like for no reason. I think they might have been scared of me before. And also, I coach Little League. This mindfulness stuff is great for baseball. I just give the kids little pointers, from the class, you know like 'Feel the bat,' 'Feel your feet,' 'Breathe,' and wow, what a difference!"

It's time to bring out Stress Organ Guy. Together with dry-erase markers we color in all the places where we feel stress, basically *all* the colorful organs that Hugh depicted. And I review the fight, flight, or freeze response, our primitive survival wiring that may not serve so well with our modern-day stressors, as we've heard in the class with Eileen.

Then we get to what we call external and internal stressors, and the way we cope with them. They've already listed their external stressors early on—health issues, family, finances, work, traffic...—as well as some of our less healthy coping strategies, such as food, alcohol, drugs, or overwork. We talk about how using these keeps us stuck in stress reactivity.

Now, regarding internal stressors, here comes the really interesting part. "Imagine that between your thumb and index finger is a juicy wedge of lemon," I say. "Imagine seeing the sections, the color, smelling the citrusy smell, feeling the rind. Now bring it toward your mouth like you are going to bite into it." I pause. "What's happening?"

"Salivating," many voices say. I look around, seeing puckered mouths and grins. Imaginary lemons are in the air everywhere held up by their fingers. Even I am salivating.

"We can produce a physical response to an imaginary lemon. Why is this relevant?"

"Well, Eileen gave a perfect example when she said she felt her heart racing on the way to the principal's office but nothing had happened yet," June says. "And sometimes that happens to me when I am trying to go to sleep. I start thinking about things from the past or the next day and my heart pounds too. I get all revved up."

"What makes your heart pound?"

"My thoughts and fears and previous experiences!" she replies.

"This is what we mean by internal stressors. Our thoughts are connected to our bodies and so our thoughts can and do trigger stressful responses. That's why people come in to meditation thinking they want this quiet mind with no thoughts, which is pretty impossible. A quiet mind is helpful, but not necessarily our goal; in fact aiming for it can produce the opposite. Have you noticed that? The practice is really about seeing what our minds are up to and then seeing how they make us feel and act. Getting 'on to ourselves,' as Joe so beautifully put it."

Zach tentatively raises his hand. "I have to be honest with you, Beth. I do get some relief when I am doing the practices, and like I said I have seen a few more pleasant moments. But in the last few years some really big and horrible stuff has happened in our family." He glances at his mom. "And I still don't feel like I can face it. I just want to keep the door closed, but then again..." he chokes a little, "I get flashes of it. It's pretty terrifying."

In the intervening weeks since class started, Zach's mom shared with me the enormous family tragedy that had brought them to the class. Zach's father and aunt were killed in a car accident, and Zach was called to the scene because he was the only one home. Needless to say, this was extremely traumatic for him, and for the whole family. We've talked about the possibility of therapy, and he is quite resistant after trying it a few times. I tread carefully with Zach and at the same time I know that he is very strong.

"I really appreciate your sharing that, Zach. How does it feel to talk about it right now?"

"I'm nervous, I've got that heart pounding thing those guys were talking about."

"May I ask you a question?"

"Sure, okay."

"What do you do when the flashes happen?"

"I just, um...I guess I distract myself. I get busy. I might go on Facebook or text someone about, you know, just trivial stuff. Or I go outside if I'm home and shoot some hoops."

"It sounds like you are really aware of what is going on, and that you're good at taking care of yourself. In my experience these really difficult things take their own time. It takes a lot of courage just to practice at all and then to talk about it. Would you be willing to keep doing that and see what happens?"

"Yeah. I really like my peeps here anyway. And that helps." He smiles. You can feel people leaning in to support him without actually interfering in his process.

There is something I need to be clear on, for myself and for Zach. I don't need to help Zach or fix him, but I am here to support him and stay in very close contact with him. And for all our talk about "turning toward" our difficulties, there is a time and place for this *and* a pace. I completely respect his process at this point. His own wisdom tells him that it is kind and compassionate to go shoot some hoops or connect with a friend. That is, simply put, wise. If I think he's in trouble, then that is another story, but I am not seeing that right now. I see someone really courageous. I will stay in touch with him and continue to see if therapy becomes a possibility.

The Fourth Noble Truth: Showing Up and Practicing Is the Path to Ending Suffering!

The participants in an MBSR program are on a path, they've committed to two and a half hours a week for eight weeks and an all-day retreat on a Saturday. They've committed to practicing some form of meditation forty-five minutes to an hour a day. You could say the practice is the path and the awareness that arises from the practice is the way to freedom. In fact, it *is* freedom. We can see this in the sharing this week—that people are continuing to glimpse options and space in their lives. They are practicing and experiencing a reduction in suffering. The Buddha's teaching offers a path also, which is described in the Fourth Noble Truth—the Eightfold Path.

Before we actually get into exploring the Eightfold Path, I'd like to mention a few things. All the eight factors in that Path are preceded by the Pali word *samma*. *Samma* is often translated as "right," but this is not right as opposed to wrong, as we might use it in the West. I prefer the translation of "wise, wholesome, or complete." Going forward I will use the word "wise."

The Fourth Noble Truth as described by the Buddha outlines the instructions he gave for a way of living he found that alleviates or ends *dukkha* or suffering. It's called the Eightfold Path because it consists of eight ways of being and doing that we can practice:

1. Wise View: insight into the true nature of reality.

2. Wise Intention: cultivating renunciation, good will, and harmlessness.

3. Wise Speech: using speech compassionately.

4. Wise Action: ethical conduct, manifesting compassion.

5. Wise Livelihood: making a living through ethical and nonharmful means.

6. Wise Effort: cultivating wholesome qualities, releasing unwholesome qualities.

7. Wise Mindfulness: whole body-and-mind awareness.

8. Wise Concentration: through meditation practice seeing deeply into the nature of reality, with stability of mind-heart.

Please note, this path is not a step-by-step "how to" manual. It is not linear, although the practice of one certainly supports another. It is not like the magazines in our waiting rooms: "Five steps to a happier you." "Six steps to a flatter belly." Rather, it is more like a spiral or a double helix, like a strand of DNA. It's hard to tell the inside from the outside, and all the parts feed into and inform one another. They also strengthen one another, like a rope that is stronger with many strands.

Throughout the rest of the book we will be looking at the Eightfold Path. I do not follow it in exact sequence, but rather as I see it unfolding in the MBSR classroom we're joining here.

Wise View

The first step of the Eightfold Path is Wise View. This makes sense because it would be very difficult to move anywhere without such a view. We couldn't travel the path if we couldn't see a direction. We don't have to see the whole thing, just somewhere to start. Where I live in the mountains, the cloud layer lands right at our elevation sometimes and it's hard to see the road or even the car. Practicing without a wise view might be like trying to drive in the cloud. Classically, Wise View means simply that you have seen for yourself the Four Noble

Truths—the truth that there is suffering, that there is a cause of suffering, that there is an end to suffering, and that there is a path leading to that end. See what I mean about the teachings folding back on each other?

It begins with seeing or understanding the Four Noble Truths, because to be motivated to find a "cure" you must acknowledge that you are actually suffering. This may seem obvious, but surprisingly it often isn't. In medical practice it is quite astounding to see what people tolerate, and the degree to which human beings can adapt to discomfort. The early stress physiologists called this the disease of adaptation. Sometimes, of course, we have to adapt, like someone with a spinal cord injury and subsequent quadriplegia. However, there are types of suffering that we shouldn't just adapt to, because they can be addressed and alleviated, at least somewhat. But it does take time and effort. When patients are diagnosed with diabetes or depression, we don't (hopefully) simply give them a pill or an injection. We educate them about the many things they can do to enhance their health. So, too, the Buddha is saying in this Fourth Noble Truth that to have a life with less suffering and more freedom, we have to practice certain things. The first practice is seeing clearly the nature of our suffering and our relationship to it.

I believe everyone who comes to MBSR already has Wise View. Part of that view is to ask questions like, "Is there another way than the way I have been approaching life?" They've already asked that question or they would not have signed up for class. And they already have had some space around their suffering or they would not be able to sit in the circle and name it. The curiosity and awareness they are beginning to have, which I wrote about in chapter 3 and am continuing to discuss here, are indicators of this clarity.

Early on in the MBSR program we're asked to consider that feeling stressed and having "stressors" is only part of the equation. We are invited to begin to look at the way we look at things and how that affects us, which we've seen in the Pleasant Events Calendar and the Unpleasant Events Calendar and the sharing in the class. This lays the groundwork for where Joe is in class 4—when he is seeing that his point of view is harmful to his relationship and that his partner has a different point of view that might need to be considered. This new view is a wise view.

The Third Foundation of Mindfulness— Mindfulness of Mind

The Third Foundation of Mindfulness is Mindfulness of Mind. Here we really need to pay attention to what in the Buddha's time was meant by the Pali term *citta*, lest you think it has only to do with the thing inside your skull. A translation of *citta* is: mind *and* heart. To establish mindfulness of *citta*, we're practicing awareness of mental states, *including* emotions and the connections between mental states and emotions.

The Buddha is very specific in his instructions. For example, he asks that we know "an angry mind to be angry and a mind without anger to be without anger, a contracted mind to be contracted and a distracted mind to be distracted, a great mind to be great and a narrow mind to be narrow." The list is quite extensive. He really wants us to get curious and familiar with these diverse mind states.

I so appreciate the matter-of-factness he brings to this. There is no judgment, just a vivid list of the myriad ways the mind states simply *are* from time to time, another naming of the human condition which welcomes us all.

As with the awareness of feeling tone in chapter 3, it's nonjudgmental awareness that is so important here. If we have some familiarity with and awareness of a particular mind-heart state, we're much less likely to get swept away by and lost in it. This doesn't mean that we don't—or shouldn't—have angry, distracted, or narrow mind states. The teaching simply suggests that we should know them for what they are, as well as not miss the moments when the mind is not distracted, when the mind is clear.

By this point in the program, people in the class are beginning to know something about their minds and the mind-body connection. Eileen, for instance, anticipated a certain interaction in the principal's office, she has some thoughts about this, and she knows she has these thoughts and that they affect her body because she is able to describe it to us. She is aware of what her mind is doing. She's not alone. In the sitting meditation, many people were aware of their thoughts. This means they are not completely lost in them.

When Joe says "Joe is on to Joe," he is experiencing the Third Foundation. He knows his angry mind and body are angry and rigid and he is also aware of something in him larger than that state, something we might call wisdom or clarity, which opens up possibilities for new behavior. Zach is having much greater awareness of what his mind is doing. Alan knows busy mind to be busy and Eileen knows worried mind to be worried. They are seeing their mind states more clearly.

Awareness Is the Beginning of Freedom

This awareness of what the mind is up to, and how we feel when certain thoughts arise, is the beginning of freedom from habitual patterns that cause us to suffer. Here's an example from my own life. There is a particular mind-body condition that I have learned to be very "on to" because it has caused me no end of trouble. It's what I call "tired mind." When I'm fatigued physically or mentally, my mind gets panicky and starts listing all the things I have to do, even going months into the future, as well as bringing up long-stalled projects I haven't yet done, like cleaning the garage. This thought pattern sends me into a panic. If I catch it early on, noting, "Oh, here's tired mind wanting me to save (and clean) the world..." and then perhaps stop for a minute, I don't spin out. I may even make a wise and kind decision to rest, and come back to my lists later.

Of course, tired mind is not the only difficult mind state. There is also hungry mind (being with me when I have low blood sugar is not fun) and lonely mind. In fact there is a useful acronym from the 12-step recovery programs to help people be aware of times when they may be vulnerable to drinking or using, but they are useful for us all. The acronym is H.A.L.T., which stands for Hungry, Angry, Lonely, and Tired. Being aware of these mind-body-heart states as they are occurring allows us to address the actual issue directly, rather than indirectly through an addictive, destructive behavior.

In MBSR, in or around class 4, through the body scan, sitting meditation, and educational components on stress reactivity, participants are beginning to get "on to" themselves. Through regular practice we begin to develop this kind and supportive knowing what the mind-body-heart is doing and feeling. We start to increase our ability to see stressful reactions for what they are, and perhaps also to see the forms of "maladaptive coping" that go along with them. New choices are beginning to open for some people, while others are noticing habitual patterns in a new way without changing anything.

One of the challenges for both student and teacher at this particular point in the curriculum is that we are asked to simply catch these critical moments and hold them in awareness, without doing anything about them. We allow the knowing to be the medicine itself, without adding anything. We are asked to simply continue to practice. This takes great courage on the part of both student and teacher. Everyone came into the program with great courage already in abundance, but it also takes a certain amount of steadiness and stability. The practices done on a regular basis foster this steadiness. It also takes time, which is why we don't invite it until week four.

The Zen tradition has a story about Bodhidharma, who brought Buddhism from India to China and is considered the First Ancestor of Zen. It illustrates this teaching. It is said that as he sat in meditation facing a stone wall, an eager student stood in the snow asking and asking for help. What did he want? He wanted Bodhidharma to calm his mind. He begged, "Please give me peace of mind." Bodhidharma is said to have replied, "Bring me your mind and I will pacify it for you." The student cried, "I have searched for it everywhere and I cannot find it!" Bodhidharma replied, "Then I have already pacified it for you!"

In my early years of Zen practice, I sat many retreats at Yokoji Zen Mountain Center. During these retreats students have the good fortune to meet individually with our teacher Tenshin Roshi. I would meditate for a period and then go in and tell him how terrible I was doing. "My mind never stops, I am always thinking."

"And what is your relationship to that thinking?"

My initial reaction was to say to him, "What do you mean? I hate it and I'm a bad meditator." However, there was something about the question and the patient, nonjudgmental way he asked it that caught my attention. Over and over I would try to bring him my mind and all its antics to have it pacified, to stop my thinking, and over and over he would point me gently away from the activity of the mind to my relationship to my mind, which at the time was critical and evaluative. Like water wearing down stone, his unwavering presence and kind questions wore at my strong identification with my mind, and slowly I began to relate to it without so much reactivity. I began to have a kinder, more spacious relationship with my mind, and guess what? It liked that and quieted down. Tenshin Roshi modeled that relationship for me and invited that curiosity so that eventually I could do it for myself.

The Buddha's teachings on Mindfulness of Mind also ask us to know and to see the "arising and passing away" of our emotional mind states, which is repeated in the refrain of the *Discourse on the Four Foundations of Mindfulness* I've written about previously. A phrase borrowed from the Bible is also used to help people in recovery, and frequently heard in the MBSR classroom: "This too shall pass." Sustained attention and turning toward experiences are what make consciousness of this truth possible. We come to see that every sensation, every thought, arises and disappears. Here we see the teaching on impermanence again. While the realization that all things change can sometimes be challenging, it can also offer us great freedom. I invite you to see how bringing awareness to the truth of impermanence functions in your life and how it may offer you this taste of liberation from time to time.

Chapter 5

THE DHARMA OF CHOICE:
Finding a Bigger Container

I'm standing out on the back patio of my house with my green down jacket on, sipping hot dark coffee and feeling the cold mountain air on my face. I see ribbons of orange and gold through the green of the pines where the oaks are turning their leaves beautiful fall colors. At our mountain home in early November we feel the approach of winter. Last night we had the wood stove going and I wore wool socks to bed. It's a wild place up here; our two acres adjoin 100 acres of wilderness and national forest. There aren't many houses and the landscape is untamed.

Although it's only thirty miles away, I know as I head to work in Palm Springs, the town will be very different in many ways. Desert instead of mountains, cactus instead of pines, heat instead of cold, strip malls instead of trees. I chop firewood, wearing steel-toed boots at home, and wear sandals and work on a computer in the office. The contrasts in my life from mountain to desert remind me that life isn't just one way and neither am I. In class tonight we'll also be moving into a different and wider way of practicing and seeing.

As I enter the office I see that the Halloween decorations on the front door have changed—from a skeleton and cobwebs to a turkey in a pilgrim hat. The conversations with the staff have changed from kids' costumes to recipes for Thanksgiving.

I love these discussions as they balance the intensity of patient care with the sustaining aspects of our everyday lives.

Today I see my patient Arthur, age eighty-two, who never comes without gifts for the staff. He might bring a copy of *Vanity Fair* for Angela, a Japanese fan for Chris, and some cookies for Marcie. Knowing about our shared love of birds, he once brought me a plastic birdbath from Walmart. It sits in the front of my house under a pine tree and is a favorite hangout for two pairs of redheaded woodpeckers that he loves hearing about. I feel Arthur's presence all the time.

Expecting him to ask me about the woodpeckers, as he usually does, I see right away that he has tears in his eyes. "I am being moved to assisted living and won't be able to bring Louie or Rocky," his rescued dogs that he adores. He chokes with sorrow. I roll the stool over quite close to him and put my arm around his shaking shoulders. There's nothing to say. Just bear witness. It is heart-breaking. I know this time has been coming; he can't take care of himself and goes in and out of the hospital. I tell him how sorry I am and we sit in silence, breathing together. I ask Angela to schedule him with me for next week. I will see him more frequently now just to stay connected.

Watching Arthur hobble out with his cane, I stand in the hall for a moment, feeling my feet on the floor and my body standing. I breathe with this broken-hearted sensation in my chest. I go to my office and sit down for a moment, seeing the piles of charts but doing absolutely nothing, just giving myself and this sadness some kind space. I know I need to keep moving, but I need a moment. I hear Angela and Marcie talking about recipes for au gratin potatoes, and I am comforted.

There are things I could do, like eat some of the leftover Almond Joy bars in the office kitchen. I could go rushing to my next patient, or check my phone or emails. I could get busy or numb. I've done all these things lots of times, but I don't today, and not very often anymore. I let all the hours of practice I've done hold me for a while before I do anything, then go into the next exam room and the next unknown thing.

As I drive to class, I'm thinking about the theme of class 5, which is creative responding through mindful awareness, that is, knowing that we're stressed *when* we're stressed through the body's signals, and making a conscious choice about how to meet that stress. I see how this response was there for me today. Pausing to allow space for my feelings made it possible for me not to go into old reactive behaviors (eating or overbusyness) when I felt sad. It did not make the situation with Arthur better, but it also did not make it worse. I didn't add to the suffering in the way I treated myself or others.

Practicing medicine can get disheartening sometimes. I am sure you sometimes feel disheartened in your life, times when you wonder: Why am I doing this? What's the point of all this work? For me, when I have these thoughts, I remind myself of my intention to alleviate suffering in any way that I can and not add to it through my own unconscious habitual behavior. Then I take the time to breathe in the moment without reacting from old habits.

The class 5 curriculum is structured so that at this midpoint we will hear from everyone, either written on the self-assessment form or, hopefully, out loud. It's a great time for me to find out how some of the quieter people are doing and see if there is any support I can provide. It feels good to be in the classroom, kicking off my sandals and seeing the rowdy row of shoes. Loafers, high heels, sneakers—a shoe sangha. I see Joe and Zach talking animatedly with one another, and wonder what they are talking about. There are other groups, too. Renée and Nikki and Elaine are gathered together. Norma and Alan are talking with Carol.

Just as we have gathered into our circle, Brian comes in with a walker, and the class erupts in applause. He smiles bashfully, waves one hand, and sits down. We've been in touch, so I already know that his surgery has gone well and that his spirits continue to rise. We sit for a moment, "arriving." We look at the room and each other, listen to sounds, feel the body, feel the breath.

We begin class 5 with standing yoga. It feels good to move my body and I can see that other people are enjoying it too. As we move, raising the arms above the head, stretching from side to side and through all the other postures, I invite a pause from time to time: "Now coming into stillness and feeling what is here to be felt. Are there any effects in the body or the mind or the emotions from what we just did?" We live at such a fast pace; we rarely stop long enough to notice the consequences of an action or even a thought.

We're building this possibility—this process—pausing and noticing, into the yoga so that folks might try it in the yoga of their lives. I recently received an email from a therapist who took the summer MBSR class that reflected this idea: "I find the yoga, especially stopping to notice the after-effects, has really changed how I go through my day. I take a moment to take stock between patients and between other activities as well, to see how I am feeling and what's called for now, before I move on. Things don't build up so much or catch me off guard."

One of the many joys of teaching MBSR is hearing how people weave these practices into their lives. Never do I say, "Why don't you try doing this in your therapy practice or in your parenting." I offer it in the formal practice and people "apply to affected area as needed," as the directions on medicinal ointments say. My students are constantly affirming the truth the Buddha saw—we're all intrinsically wise and whole.

We finish the yoga series and move into sitting posture for the seated meditation. So far we have been practicing sitting meditation for about twenty minutes at a time, in class and at home, with mostly awareness of breathing and sounds. This evening I am introducing the longer practice which will be about forty minutes long and will include other objects of attention. In addition to the breath, body sensations, and sounds, we'll focus on thoughts as objects themselves, and on emotions that may or may not be connected to those thoughts, and then open ourselves to what is called choiceless awareness. Choiceless awareness is about opening the field of awareness to allow all things to come and go as they naturally will. You can access an audio of this exercise at www.newharbinger.com/39164 (Track 5: Choiceless Awareness).

The longer sitting meditation challenges participants to work with stillness of the body, feeling sensations come and go and not reacting, as well as exploring new objects of attention that might have previously been seen as interruptions in awareness. In the written MBSR curriculum we see the word "capacity" used several times in class 5. This word really speaks to me about that we are doing now—building capacity. Capacity for what? The capacity to be with what is uncomfortable and unwanted when it's voluntary (in meditation), so that when it's not voluntary (in life) we have a greater capacity to be with it without running away or otherwise acting unconsciously. As a result of our wise effort in practicing meditation, we're more able to sit with what is, rather than do anything that might harm ourselves or others through our reactivity.

We're also developing greater curiosity about areas of experience that we might never have noticed before. What is a thought? Does it have a beginning, middle, and end? What is an emotion? The moment we bring curiosity to anything, we have already increased our capacity. We are more conscious, which opens up choices. To be curious takes courage and interest, even love. To be curious involves caring enough to ask.

Toward the end of the long meditation, I drop some reflection questions into the circle, like pebbles in a pond. "Knowing that this is the midway point, how has it been going so far? See if it is possible to answer without judging yourself, asking, like you would ask a dear friend: 'What am I learning? How is my commitment in terms of practice? Am I willing to commit to the second half of the course?' Please note that growth is nonlinear." Perhaps, dear reader, you might like to check in with yourself about your personal practice by answering these questions for yourself.

After folks have filled in the written midway assessment forms, I get them into pairs to share. Slowly the room fills with the buzz of their connections. I look over the forms as they lean toward each other, nodding and sharing. Nikki and Zach are laughing. Renée is handing Norma a Kleenex.

We come back together in the full circle. "We'll start with a volunteer and then go around from there," I say. "It's also fine to pass."

Debra, who has been fairly quiet so far, raises her hand. "When I was filling out the form, I started to laugh. I actually forgot that my neurologist referred me here for my headaches. It's not just that they are better; it's that I am getting so much more than that. I had no idea how much of my life I was missing. I mean, this might sound silly, but I really enjoy folding the laundry. And I am so much more present for my kids."

Alan, who is sitting next to her, says, "One thing this class is helping me with is taking stock of what is important while I go through cancer treatment. I have a hobby, really more of a passion, for restoring classic old cars. I just entered my 1955 Ford Thunderbird in a show up north. So Norma and I won't be here next week and we'll miss the retreat, but I'm really excited about it. I haven't felt this way since the diagnosis."

"I hate to miss class and especially the retreat, but this is important to us," Norma joins in. We can all feel what is not said: that he won't get to do it some other time.

"Last week I shared that I lost my temper with Billy," said Elaine. "It's been gnawing at me. I think maybe being in the class makes it hard to push things down and ignore them. So I realized I wanted to apologize to Billy and see if I could connect with him. When it was my turn to monitor the playground this week, I saw him straggling behind everyone, and where normally I would tell him to hurry up, I joined him and really looked at him. I could see he looked a little dirty and uncared for. My heart hurt a bit. I told him I was sorry that I lost my temper last week, and explained that I was having a hard day that day, but it was no excuse.

"He said, 'That's okay, I could tell you were bugged.' I asked him if he remembered what I was annoyed about. He said: 'Yeah, I was talking when I shouldn't have been.' We agreed that we would each work on our part and try to help each other. And then I did something I haven't done for about a zillion years. When I saw him on the swings later, I got on the one next to him and we swung together! I don't know who was more surprised, him or me. I feel like I've lost my original reason for being a teacher, I'm so stressed and overwhelmed. I feel really sad about that, but that was a good moment."

I ask, "When your heart opened toward Billy, what was it that you noticed?"

"That he seems like a neglected child who acts out to get attention. And I felt like scooping him up."

"I'm wondering if you feel like that toward yourself at all."

She tears up a little. "I have been neglecting myself and I don't ask for help. This class is the first self-care I've done in a while. I guess Billy and I have something in common." She places her hands on her heart and we sit in silence for a few moments.

Zach says, "I've noticed that I'm starting to do things I used to like before everything happened, before my dad and aunt died." It's the first time he's said anything specific about the family tragedy. "I played my guitar a little bit and got on my bike."

Joe says, "I'm sleeping better and I don't have to drive around the block to see if the garage door is closed, because I was present when I did it! My partner thinks the class is doing something for me, he practically pushed me out of the door tonight!" Joe looks like a different person than the one who yelled at me a few weeks ago.

Lisette says, "I lost eight pounds and I don't even know how. I guess it's the mindful eating plus meditating. I don't think I reach for food as much from stress." She and Raúl are holding hands. He says: "This has been good for us to do together." They smile at each other.

For people to show up every week and become genuinely interested in their experience and do this longer sitting meditation with more silence, without running out of the room, they have to have some connection to their original intention for coming to MBSR, whatever that was for each one of them. And in order to challenge themselves, they need to apply some effort. Not so much effort that they fall over with the strain, but not so little that they go to sleep. In the guided reflection at about the halfway point of the class, they have a chance to reconnect with their initial intention and then ask themselves, "What kind of effort am I willing to make for the remainder of the class, to support that intention?" Also, in class 5 people are seeing that they have the possibility to make choices that perhaps go against their habitual reactive behavior, and to respond creatively. In order for that to happen, they must have the intention to do so and, let's face it, they must make some effort to do something a little more challenging than reaching for the Almond Joy bar or the tech device. Interestingly, where we're going in this chapter shortly are the factors of Wise Intention and Wise Effort on the Eightfold Path, but first we'll talk about the Fourth Foundation of Mindfulness, which also includes these factors.

The Fourth Foundation of Mindfulness: Mindfulness of Dharmas, or Our Life Is Our Teacher

In class 5 and in examining the factors of the Eightfold Path, we are bringing awareness to more and more areas of our lives and have the opportunity to see things from a different and perhaps wider perspective. The Fourth Foundation of Mindfulness, which is Mindfulness of Dharmas, invites us to bring curiosity and kind attention to everything that may offer us a teaching. The word *Dharma* literally means the teachings of the Buddha, and it also means life, or all of reality, teaching us. When we learn from our own experiences in life, we can be awakened. What do I mean by awakened? We're present to our lives, to other living beings, and to the great earth itself, and see clearly our relationship to them and our effect on them. The world teaching us is also Dharma. We may be awakened by our encounter with the sound of the wind, the shadows on a rock, a child's voice, or even the other people in the same traffic jam we are in, because we have a sense of our interconnectedness. We know we're not alone, even if we seem to be going in different directions.

If you look at the classic texts, establishing mindfulness in the realm of the Dharmas includes specific lists of the Buddha's teachings. Remember what I said in the last chapter about the way the teachings fold back upon and weave in and among each other? Guess what one of the lists is? Yep, the Four Noble Truths, which includes the Eightfold Path. Here we will cover two aspects of the latter: Wise Intention and Wise Effort.

Wise Intention: Renunciation, Good Will, and Compassion

In discussing Wise Intention, the Buddha suggested that we practice with three areas of intention. The first is the intention of renunciation. Renunciation is not a word we use much in the West. Maybe, we think, it applies only to monks and nuns. But in a culture and time pushing us toward having more and doing more, forming an intention to give something up—to simplify—is worth exploring. Once, at the end of an orientation talk on MBSR, after I spoke about the kind of time commitment it takes to participate in the program, a woman said, "I can see if I am going to do this, I am going to have to give up something else." I was struck by the wisdom and foresight in this, because often we think, "Can't I just cram one more thing in? I don't want to give anything up!" I talk about this in class 1, asking participants, "What would you be willing to let go of in order to make the time to meditate? Watch a little less television? Not check Facebook so often? Simplify in some small or large way?" The question, besides being practical and realistic, speaks to the practice of renunciation.

Today when I was stressed at work, you could say I practiced renouncing Almond Joy bars in the service of my larger intention, which is to be healthy and to feel my feelings. I've learned that if I do *not* practice renunciation and I overeat or overwork, I still have the original sadness or stress to deal with in addition to a feeling of regret that I made a choice that may add to my suffering. When I can see this through and renounce, this is honoring Wise Intention.

Renunciation can be practiced in the context of the length of our meditations as well. Often people ask, "Can't I meditate for a shorter time?" Perhaps they're hoping to fit meditation into a hectic day. The answer is yes, you can, it's always better to do some than none. But the benefits of sustaining attention over longer periods of time are profound. I have found that if we stay with our experience long enough, we can start to see cause and effect. If we're only paying attention for a few minutes, we may miss valuable information that the longer period of awareness might bring. While we might get instant gratification from the old behavior, afterward we might feel pretty crummy and actually regret that we did it. We get this vital feedback loop if we're paying some sustained attention. This sort of learning—of coming to know what else is possible when we make the effort—is where practicing mindfulness begins to lead to behavior change. The changes come in what may seem like small moments, but these moments, as Jon Kabat-Zinn says, are "not small, they're life!"

Letting go is not about deprivation, really, it's about feeling whole and free of regret. In the classical teachings, freedom from regret is a precursor to joy. I've tried this idea out a lot in the laboratory of me and it bears out. Lack of regret is in fact a form of joy. Who knew?

Is there anything you'd be willing to let go of in the service of your own and others' greater good?

Good Will and Compassion—Cultivating Our Natural Way of Being

The other two areas of Wise Intention the Buddha suggested we cultivate are good will and compassion. These are intended to counteract ill will or thoughts generated by anger, aversion, and cruelty. With practice, we actively water the seeds of loving-kindness and compassion in ourselves and we are more likely to be aware when ill will arises.

There are two active ways you can practice these aspects of Wise Intention. The first aspect is called Loving-Kindness Meditation or Metta. Metta is a Pali word that also translates as "boundless friendliness." Metta is the wish for all beings to be happy and free from suffering, and the practice lies in the heartfelt offering of this wish to yourself and others. The second aspect is compassion or Karuna practice, defined as the quivering of the heart which occurs when our good will meets suffering. Metta or Loving-Kindness is good will under all conditions. Karuna—compassion—addresses more specifically what happens in the heart when our wish for well-being encounters someone, including ourselves, who is suffering. We can cultivate it to grow with intention and practice. We explore both of these practices in great detail in chapter 10. You can also find both written and audio guidance at www.newhar

binger.com/39164. (For written guidance, click "Practicing the Immeasurables with Phrases." For audio guidance, click "Track 6: Metta" and "Track 7: Karuna.")

One of the things that is so interesting about MBSR is that we teach ways of paying attention and we practice this a lot! Then we see the positive qualities of kindness and compassion come forth. Through her practice, Elaine is reconnecting with her original intention to nurture children's education and lives. She knows she has lost something, and she is "turning toward" this difficulty. The pain of feeling disconnected and the awareness of the harm it causes led her, this week, to take a moment to really look at Billy and feel compassion. When she saw that he is a child who is perhaps suffering from neglect, she practiced loving-kindness by apologizing to him and then getting on the swings with him.

In Elaine's experience you may recognize an example of the Third Foundation of Mindfulness—Mindfulness of Mind (or of mind-heart states). In order to take a different course, she had to first be aware of the mind state she was in. Then, without judgment but hopefully with kindness and compassion for herself, she practiced spaciousness, responding to her student from her heart, which *is* love and compassion.

Wise Effort: Moving Toward Peace and Away from Suffering

Wise Effort is another step on the Eightfold Path. Here's the simplest, most direct way I can describe it: According to the Buddha's teachings, Wise Effort leads toward freedom, peace, and contentment, and away from greed, anger, and ignorance—in short, away from suffering.

The teachings on Wise Effort ask us to investigate if what we are doing, saying, and thinking, which are our efforts, are leading to wholesome states of mind-heart or to unwholesome ones. This word "wholesome," like the word "renunciation," might not be terribly appealing. For me, growing up in the late fifties and early sixties, it brings to mind television shows like *Father Knows Best* and *Leave It to Beaver*. These shows, so different from my own life, left me feeling that what I was experiencing in my house and in my young life was highly abnormal and certainly unwholesome. If you have negative associations with that word, see if you can find language that allows you to explore the concept without preconceptions. All that is being pointed to is an invitation to be curious and open about what certain efforts lead to. So what word works for you? Personally I like the words "freedom" and "wholeness." Are your efforts bringing more or less freedom? More or less wholeness?

The Buddha's story is a great example of Wise Effort. He had the intention to awaken, to be liberated from the unnecessary suffering caused by craving. He put a tremendous amount of effort and energy into the ascetic pathway and was told he was a master. But it didn't do anything to answer his fundamental angst. It did not offer a lasting or sustainable peace, and it weakened him so much that he was of no use to anyone, including himself. In this way, his effort was not wise. However, because he did not give up, we could say it was a stepping stone to the path we are on today. So I wouldn't say it was wasted.

In MBSR we are inviting Wise Effort right from the beginning. If we are going to put energy into healing through MBSR, it means taking two and half hours per week for the class and an hour a day for meditation. That might mean we're going to have to stop putting energy into other things that do not lead to health and wholeness. That is, we're going to have to practice some degree of "renunciation." We continue to foster Wise Effort when we do mindful yoga, asking people to pay careful attention to how far they go, and how long they go, noticing the signals of the body as well as the messages from the mind. I might say, "If your neck veins are popping out and your jaw is clenched, you might want to consider your effort." I go on to suggest a couple of ways to check with one's effort in yoga, as in life: Can you breathe easily and freely in the pose, or in your life? And could you potentially turn up the corners of your mouth? I am not saying you *should* smile, I'm just saying to be aware of whether you *could* smile.

In the body scan and in the sitting meditation we try to bring the mind "gently but firmly" back to the present moment. This takes energy and effort. Sometimes people will say after a practice period, with great surprise, "That was a lot of work!" At this point we can investigate if that "work" led to a feeling of inadequacy—if they were striving for a certain outcome and didn't get it, or if they were doing the diligent work of training the attention and found it worthwhile, if not easy.

In daily life, practicing Wise Effort might look like this. Let's say I've had a hard day at work. I want to lie on the couch and stream my latest BBC murder mystery. I am aware that my nervous system is activated and my mind is full of the day's difficulties. I want to numb out. Now, as I've said earlier, I pretty much know where that will lead—it won't lead me away from suffering, especially if it is a particularly grisly murder! I'll still have the feelings; I'll just have been distracted for a while.

So using Wise Intention and Wise Effort, I go for a walk instead, and take in my surroundings. I could walk and let my mind run wild, but from practice I have a choice to walk with awareness. I feel my feet, feel the air on my face, and listen to the evening birdsong. During dinner I connect with Hugh and we each share parts of our day. After dinner I do a short body scan and check in again. What now? I might feel the pull to check emails or go on Facebook. Now I ask myself again where this behavior is likely to lead. Frankly, it's like Russian Roulette. It might be just fine. I might have lovely messages from friends, or find out it is someone's birthday. Or there could be an overwhelming demand for my services, people expressing political views that are upsetting, or one of those emails that comes with a red exclamation point next to it. (Yech!) Knowing how vulnerable I am to any additional stress based on my day and my present-moment awareness, I can exercise Wise Effort and decide to renounce or minimize some or all of these impulses and make the choice not to go online.

In the traditional teachings we are also invited to pay attention to where our mind efforts go. Are we nursing resentment? Are we rehearsing an interaction we anticipate will be difficult, while we miss what is right in front of us? Can we use sustained awareness to ask ourselves: where is this thought-stream leading? And then choose a more wholesome direction? For people suffering from depression and anxiety, this awareness of how one thought can lead to a cascade of thoughts, escalating to despair or panic, can be a vital awareness and choice point.

How do we know if our effort is wise? Applying the Four Foundations of Mindfulness:

- Mindfulness of the Body lets me know how stressed I really am.

- Mindfulness of Feeling Tones and Mindfulness of Mind-Heart States gives me information about where I am mentally and emotionally.

- Mindfulness of Dharmas reminds me that all beings suffer, so there is nothing wrong with having a hard day. It happens. And it also helps me remember that craving (television, ice cream, a technology fix) leads to *more* suffering, and from previous experience (not theory) I realize that there is the possibility of freedom from suffering, a freedom I have tasted many times. The way to enter that freedom is through applying Wise View, Wise Intention, and Wise Effort.

Now, how much effort is Wise Effort? Well, the Buddha was a master of analogies because he taught so many different kinds of students. There's a story about his interaction with a lute-playing monk regarding this question. The monk wants to know how much effort to put in his practice. The Buddha asks, "What happens when the string of your instrument is too loose?"

"When you pluck it, the sound is not clear," replies the monk.

"What happens when the string is too taut?"

"It will likely break."

"The practice of the Way is the same," said the Buddha. "Find the right amount of tautness and looseness and the sound will be as it should be."

We can be attuned to our effort in the same way the lute player is attuned to the sound of the strings. No one can tell you exactly what the balance is. You have to find it for yourself. Play with this effort in your practice and see how it is for you. Participants in the MBSR class are working with this now. Zach shared that he is starting to do things that make him feel alive and whole, which he has not done since his great loss. Nikki shared that she is being kinder to herself and others. Wisdom unfolding indeed.

Chapter 6

THE DHARMA OF OUR SPEECH:
The Lessons of Relationship and Community

Perhaps because I know that tonight's MBSR class will focus on the particular stress inherent in our communications with other people, I am more aware of that realm with my patients today. One thing I have learned the hard way over the years is how important it is for our team in the medical office not to complain or gossip about patients, especially the ones who are really difficult to deal with. Otherwise we can really wind each other up about someone, reinforcing the idea that they are a pain, especially that they are a pain to *us*, rather than acknowledging that they are *in* pain.

Being mindful of the impact of our speech, my team and I attempt to avoid an atmosphere of "us against them." We try to speak in such a way as to lead to a more positive outcome—even if that means setting a strong boundary. We share important background information that may deeply inform our interactions or otherwise affect the person's health, such as: her husband is in jail, or her child was in an accident, or he just lost his job. We come up with a plan to deal with someone who is unreasonably demanding pain medication or who is simply rude. So as Angela and I go through the schedule together this morning and I see a particularly difficult patient's name on the schedule (difficult in that he is always asking for Vicodin and Xanax), we just look at each other and say nothing, until she says, "Want to make some coffee?"

Today the importance of how we communicate was brought home to me when I saw a couple I love—robust, warm people with six adult children and bunches of grandchildren, retired from their kitchen supply business. I usually see them separately, but today they were in the exam room together, both charts stacked neatly on top of each other. Gino is going through prostate cancer treatment and I wanted an update, so we started with him.

"How are you, Gino? What's new?"

"I'm fine, everything is fine."

"It's not fine!" Marcella joins in. "You're exhausted, you're nauseated and—"

"Hey, it's my appointment!"

I squeeze into the conversation. "I'm looking at Dr. Solomon's notes here. He says you're responding to treatment, and that you have ten weeks to go. Is that what you recall?"

"I thought he said you were going to have to get those seed implant things," says Marcella loudly.

"I have them already! Right, Doc?" Now Gino's voice is raised.

"Hey guys," I say. "Let's calm down, we're all on the same side here."

They look at me like I'm nuts, look at each other, smile broadly, and simultaneously throw their hands in the air saying, "We're Italian!" In other words, there is no problem, this is their communication style, and for them it is a conversation. It's only me that thinks it is an argument.

They could just as easily have named any number of other cultures. The main thing is that they have revealed to me something I know about myself. I am incredibly averse to conflict. The slightest raise of a voice and my alarm bells go off.

The only person in the room who needs to calm down is me. I am able to do this with some mindful breathing, which is made easier by the fact that they have such good humor. One minute we're talking about cancer treatment and the next moment we're all laughing at ourselves.

As this couple reminds me, it's helpful to know something about our relational patterns, which is what we'll be exploring tonight in class 6. It's good to know where the patterns come from and what they feel like when they are operating, and then to have some options of response. Tonight, before I even raise the topic of mindfulness and relationships, I will listen for what the participants' practice is teaching them about communication, and I look forward to learning from them—what happens when they "apply mindfulness as needed to the affected area."

As we gather together, I am very aware of Alan and Norma's absence, and I remind the group that they are at the car show. It's clear from the response how much they care about them and each other.

We begin with yoga, followed by the longer sitting meditation with the various objects of attention that we learned the week before and in chapter 5. This evening there will be more silence and less instruction. I'm eager to hear how they did with it this week.

After forty-five minutes of meditation, I ring the bell. Then I invite them to get together in pairs and share their experience of this meditation, both this evening and from practicing with it during the week. I emphasize that in this interaction they are encouraged to practice mindful listening, as if it was also a meditation practice—which it is.

"As your partner shares, see if you can simply listen with your whole body. Noticing when your mind goes off, perhaps comparing or rehearsing what you're going to say, or thinking about something else entirely, and then kindly but firmly come back to listening. Please try not to interrupt, chime in, ask questions, or even comment when you relate to something. And when you are speaking, notice how it is to speak and be listened to."

Often people find this listening practice revolutionary, strange, wonderful, or even impossible. They discover they can't just listen in silence, can't refrain from having a conversation. No matter how it goes, it's illuminating.

After they are done with the sharing in pairs, I say, "How was that for you? You may share about the sitting practice, or the mindful listening, and anything you noticed during the week related to practice."

Jean says, "Mindful listening was hard! I wanted so much to join in, ask questions, and tell Debbie how much I relate."

"So how did you work with that?"

"I noticed it, and I almost said something, but I came back to feeling my body and my breath, and then I would focus on her again. I'm not sure I could do this all the time, or even if I would want to!"

"I understand, it can feel a bit awkward and even artificial. This really is a practice to see what it feels like, then you can play with it with more flexibility in your life. How was it to be listened to in that way?"

"Well, now that you mention it, I found I said things I might not have gotten to if she had said something."

"I realized I've already started doing this with my teenage daughter," Debbie adds. "Until recently I was so primed to do battle with her, because she is always pushing boundaries these days. But lately I have been letting her finish a sentence all the way through." She smiles. "And sometimes there's no big deal going on. We seem to be working things out with a little more ease and I'm not even sure how it happened. Maybe just by listening to her she doesn't feel she has to fight as hard."

I notice Carol and Zach looking at each other knowingly.

"I think that is happening for us, too," says Carol.

"Anything else from the week?"

Raúl says, "People at work have been asking me what's going on. I guess I am acting really differently. I think, as I listen to you all, that maybe I am listening more, too, and I just don't say as much. I also don't get so annoyed when things go wrong. So people are saying stuff to me like, 'What are you on?'"

Joe laughs. "My biggest improvement in my relationship is just keeping my mouth shut for now. When I do, I wouldn't say things go great, but there's a lot less yelling."

Renée says, "So many people told me to take the class because meditation would help my stress level as I care for my husband and as his dementia gets worse. But I have to be on the alert for him, I feel I need to be vigilant, so deep down I didn't think I could do it, I didn't think it would work for me. But what I get from this sitting meditation in particular is that we're not shutting things out! So I can be open to sound and sensations and thoughts and still have some relaxation. I feel I can be more present to myself and him. I don't know if I am describing it very well."

I think she is describing it perfectly.

Shining Light on Patterns

As you undoubtedly have experienced yourself, relationships can bring us the most joy and richness as well as intense suffering. Today we're bringing more awareness to what is already operating in our lives with other people—the not-so-helpful habitual ways of relating, as well as the ones that are working for us.

In MBSR there are various ways to shed light on our conditioned relationship patterns. I happen to like the exercises based on the martial art form Aikido, which are featured in Jon Kabat-Zinn's *Full Catastrophe Living*. I spent ten years studying

Tae Kwon Do and even got a black belt, and I studied Aikido, too, so these body-based examples speak to me. So far they have been useful for participants, too.

I tell the class, "This evening we're going to explore our patterns around conflict and relating, not to judge them but to see them more clearly. I'm going to demonstrate these through some physical role-play, but they are intended to represent emotional, verbal, or even situational scenarios. Please bear in mind that every single one of these could be a perfectly reasonable strategy in the right circumstances. We're not looking to judge them. We simply want to see if we have an unconscious survival strategy that no longer works well for us. Once we're aware of it, and aware of our triggers, we can see if there are other things on the menu to try instead.

"I'll give you an example from my own life. I grew up with a bully. My dad was really scary when he was drunk, which was often. My older brother's strategy was to push back. I saw the resulting violence. So I went completely passive and that worked for me—until it didn't. That is to say, until I was a grownup and people actually expected me, wanted me, and perhaps at times needed me to say what I thought. More importantly, I needed me to say what I thought and to stand up for myself. So as you watch these role-plays, please see how they register in your body and if there is some recognition of something familiar—knowing that whatever you see, you, like me, developed it for a good reason. Bring some kindness to the awareness."

I ask Nikki to be my partner because we are close to the same size and she seems to be connected to her body from her athletic background. The first pattern we demonstrate is that of the passive person who would avoid conflict at any cost (my previous go-to pattern).

She comes at me with arms outstretched, not aggressively but assertively, and I collapse on a chair saying, "I'm sorry, it was my fault," over and over.

"Look familiar?" I ask.

Some nodding.

"It was awful. I couldn't bear to see you give in like that," says Elaine.

"Not to put anyone on the spot, but does anyone know that one?" I ask again.

"Yes!" says Jean.

"I hated the feeling of moving against empty air. You just disappeared on me," Nikki says.

"Okay," I say, "let's try another one."

This time when Nikki comes at me, I swiftly step to the side, leaving her again with all her momentum going forward. We do this two more times. Sometimes when I demonstrate with Hugh, on the third time, he makes horns with his fingers and paws the ground like an angry bull.

"That's a good one," says Zach. "I think it's smart to just get out of the way."

"It's true it might be a good strategy in some situations, but what about the person coming at you?"

"Well, nothing has been resolved. It feels really empty—kind of like the other one, but not so passive. It seems more passive-aggressive."

"Oh my God!" says Erica. "That is what my husband and I do. We just shut down; we don't deal with our conflicts."

Now a third scenario: Nikki and I push against each other's shoulders, shouting, "I'm right! You're wrong!" until we end up laughing. I look around the room. Some other people are laughing, while others look a bit alarmed.

"Okay now, that's familiar!" says Joe.

"Me, too," say Brian and Elaine.

"What has happened here?" I ask.

"Still no resolution."

"But it doesn't seem as empty."

"Totally unproductive."

"But there is some heat, isn't there?" I say. "Some contact? Not quite as cold and empty as the other two."

Then I go on: "Now we're going to try something that comes from the martial art Aikido. Aikido is sometimes called the art of peace or harmony; it's the art of blending with the attacker's momentum—protecting oneself while causing as little harm as possible, and even grounding the energy of someone who is unstable."

This time as Nikki comes at me, I step just slightly to the side, take hold of her arm while turning my body completely to face the direction she is going in, and move with her for a few steps. Then I gently guide us in another direction. All this happens very quickly. We repeat it in slow motion.

"How did that feel?" I ask.

"That was amazing!" says Nikki.

"We learned something like that in the Marine Corps," says Brian.

"That's called blending," I say. "What would that look like in a verbal or emotional situation? In other words, how would you blend with someone who was upset with you?"

"Well, you moved toward them and then turned to see things from their point of view," says Lisette.

"Yeah," says Zach, "you tried to see it their way."

"And then?"

"You got them to see it another way."

"So I guess you'd start by really listening, like we did earlier," joins in Renée. "Also, I noticed that you started by moving toward her, but to the side so you wouldn't take the hit, but you were also saying, in effect, 'I'm willing to meet you.'"

Beautifully said.

I remind them: "Please don't get the idea that blending is always right. This demonstration is really about making what may be unconscious conscious. And with our practices, particularly the body scan and mindfulness of thoughts and feelings, we can see options and make choices that we might not have seen before. This takes some courage because it is a leap into the unknown. I've had couples tell me they've been locked into a communication pattern for years. And for some reason it's often in the car."

People laugh.

I continue: "He backs out and she says, 'Be careful!' and he says what he always says. They might as well hit 'Play' on a tape recorder. Then one day, after some practice, one of them notices the stress in their bodies and pauses, and now they're off script. It's an improvisation! If we're truly in the moment, we're always improvising. We don't have to play out the whole three acts the way we always have done in the past."

Wise Speech

In the MBSR class we're talking about communication. In the Buddha's teaching this is called Wise Speech, another component of the Eightfold Path. The Buddha had some fairly simple, direct instructions about Wise Speech. Often the instructions come in the form of what we should *not* say. I love this acronym from meditation teacher Sylvia Boorstein: W.A.I.T. Why Am I Talking? Just as Wise Intention starts with some suggestions about restraint, so, too, when addressing Wise Speech, the Buddha suggested that we refrain from false speech (tell the truth); that we refrain from divisive speech (if you don't have something constructive and purposeful to say, don't say it); that we refrain from harsh speech (be kind and warm in words and tone); and that we abstain from idle chatter (consider the necessity and timing of what you are talking about). Does it sound a lot like some of the lessons you might have been taught as a young child?

As we move into the teaching on Wise Speech on the Eightfold Path, using the Four Foundations of Mindfulness to support us, all of what we've been learning so far starts to come together. Wise Speech starts with awareness, and most importantly, listening. We also establish mindfulness inside ourselves, our body sensations of reactivity and feeling tone—is this a pleasant, unpleasant, or neutral interaction? We become aware of our mind state. Is there an angry mind? A distracted mind? And there is Mindfulness of Dharmas: where do suffering, craving, and aversion play a role here? Can I see the possibility of *Nibbana* or space? Can I bring some friendliness or compassion through my wise intention to the situation? Am I making assumptions and falling into old patterns?

My teacher Tenshin Roshi often refers to Wise Speech as the part of the path where practice "becomes real," or rather, where we make practice real. Wise Speech is referred to as one of the ethical factors of the Eightfold Path. Ethics (in Pali, *sila*) is defined as "moral principles that govern behavior." Once something is spoken or written, it's not a matter simply of beliefs, it's part of how we act in the world, and may have a great and lasting impact on others. It does in fact become real.

In the MBSR class this is why it is so helpful to explore Wise Speech in terms of behaviors and patterns. When things become more conscious, we can check and see if we are acting in accordance with our values and ethics. If we're connected to our intention to do no harm, then "blending" might come more readily. Wise Speech rests on a foundation of our ethics, and may be practiced in such a way that we are aware of the potential impact—pausing, perhaps, just long enough to consider how what we want to say may land with the other person, asking ourselves whether something we are about to say might harm our relationship, our family, or our community. Our speech is also connected to our Wise Intention—to cause no harm, or as little as humanly possible. I'll say more about a formal way we practice this in the Buddhist tradition toward the end of the chapter.

Wise Speech is where we put our Wise Intention and Wise View into the relational field. To speak it is to actualize it. If we step back and look at the wide intention of the Eightfold Path—the alleviation of suffering—we can frame our speech in this context. Will I be contributing to the greater good? Or will what I am about to say cause harm? And what is my intention? To know this we have to practice this particular way of "knowing" that we have been talking about; we need to know something about ourselves.

In meditation practice, we might get an inkling about our speech by watching the words and tone we use with ourselves and in rehearsing what we're going to say. (Come on, we all do it—rehearse conversations while meditating, right?) As we sit quietly with this nonjudgmental awareness we might get "on to ourselves," as Joe said. It is in this sustained practice that we begin to see our patterns. Without distractions we might notice any one of the patterns described in the MBSR class above. We might be aware that we are often defensive, or defeated and apologetic, or avoidant, or argumentative. We might even get a peek at where we are not truthful—maybe not an outright lie, but an exaggeration perhaps? A slight spin on the story to make ourselves look good, or even bad, or just more dramatic?

With practice we might more quickly notice the arising of reactivity in the body and know that this is a good time to pause before speaking. We may allow the stress hormones to calm down, the blood flow to return to the prefrontal cortex where we can make wise decisions. With the rapidity of communication these days, this pause is a crucial place to practice. Do you ever get one of those emails where just seeing the sender's name or the subject line sets off the fight-or-flight response?

When this happens to me, and it definitely does, I simply acknowledge it, and might even kindly note, "It's been triggered"—meaning the hormonal response. I then consider whether this is the right time to read it, and if I do and the information does not make me feel better, I know then that this is not the time to respond. I take time to let my body calm down. I may get up from my desk, do some walking meditation, have a glass of water, and often I give myself a time in which I will respond. "Okay, I'll get back to this in two days, or even two hours." This space gives me the time to investigate what is going on with me, to connect to my intention, to my heart. To prevent misunderstanding, I might let the person know: "I'll get back to you on Tuesday." This brings in the quality the Buddha spoke about in terms of considering the timing and appropriateness of our speech. In order to consider any of this, we need to have some awareness on board.

The examples from the participants in the MBSR class show how important mindful listening and pausing are. Because we're in relationships with other people a great deal of the time, that is a great place to practice. Many people find that their meditation practice sets them up really well to practice Wise Speech. As Debbie said, when she listens to her daughter all the way through she is discovering that there is not as much to argue about as she is anticipating. And for me, with those emails? Often when I actually read them, they're not going where I thought they were going. So we can also "listen" to texts, tweets, Facebook posts, and emails and really take some time before we respond.

I once had a painful misunderstanding with a dear friend that happened all through texts. I responded too quickly and was not thoughtful, we bounced off each other, and neither one of us took the time to say, "Let's just have a conversation about this!" until harm had been done. We had to work to heal this, and we did, but it was not easy. It was a really important lesson for me. Now I am a lot more like to simply call someone (like in the old days, remember?) to discuss things, because so much can get lost in these abbreviated communications.

Wise Speech in the Context of the Four Foundations of Mindfulness

While we are exploring this aspect of the Eightfold Path within the Four Noble Truths, it's also worth looking at Wise Speech through the lens of the teaching on the Four Foundations of Mindfulness, particularly the refrain that I mentioned previously. To remind you, the refrain includes the repeated instructions to see the "arising and passing away" of all phenomena. In addition, the refrain invites us to practice awareness of all Four Foundations—body, feeling tones, mind states, and Dharmas—both internally and externally. This means becoming aware of what is going on inside us and around us, moment to moment—including other people. Just as we tune in to ourselves with open curiosity, so too we practice being aware of other people's situations. Can I tune in to what is going on with them? What state are they in? Are they suffering?

With Gino and Marcella, I had some awareness of my internal reaction, I felt something was wrong. But I didn't have much external mindfulness. If I had, I might have seen that they were fine, they love each other and have a way of being together which, while different from mine, works for them! These instructions on internal and external mindfulness invite us to pay attention intentionally, nonjudgmentally, to what is going on inside us, around us, and in other beings as well. Without this flow between internal and external, our practice could become self-referential and self-involved, or too focused on the other person. Either way, we miss cues and vital information. Examples from the class show this: Elaine picked up information about her student Billy by becoming aware of him more deeply, and it opened her heart. Renée discovered that she could pay attention to her moment-to-moment experience and still be present for and to her husband suffering from Alzheimer's.

Wise Speech Is an Expression of Our Ethics

Wise Speech is one of the three ethical factors of the Eightfold Path. The other two are Wise Action and Wise Livelihood, which will be covered in chapter 8. The ethical foundations in the Buddhist teachings also come forth in what are called the precepts. Precepts are guidelines for behavior, identified across cultures and religions throughout the ages—guidelines that, when transgressed, cause great suffering and harm, and when practiced, foster peace and harmony. Depending on what Buddhist tradition you study, there may be five, ten, or more. Here are five commonly practiced ones:

- Refraining from taking life;

- Refraining from taking what is not given;

- Refraining from false speech;

- Refraining from intoxicants;

- Refraining from sexual misconduct.

Of these ethical guidelines, the Buddha said in one teaching that of all of them, being honest, "refraining from false speech," was the most important. Which is why I am discussing the precepts in this chapter.

In stating or articulating the precepts, the Buddha simply observed what human behaviors seemed to cause extreme suffering and named them in his own way. Of course these insights are not unique to Buddhism; it is likely you recognize them from your own wisdom tradition. In the Buddhist teachings they are not offered as directives or imperatives, but rather as ways of training or cultivating the mind and heart. So typically the wording might be: "I undertake the *training* to refrain from taking life or harming living beings." Or "I commit to *cultivating* not taking what is not given and to fostering an attitude of generosity." The implication of the concept of cultivating or training is that you are working on doing this, knowing that you will not do it "perfectly." Rather, you are committing to growing the capacity more and more.

In the Zen tradition we have a ceremony in which practitioners study the precepts and then, with the teacher and the sangha, commit to living them to the best of our ability. At the center where I practice, we also have a monthly day of reflection where we start the day by reading all of them and then each person chooses one to focus on for the day, while we have a "care for your temple day" that involves volunteer activities to work on the upkeep of the center. In the evening we sit in a council and share what we discovered or felt during the practice day. It's a great way to stay connected to our ethics and to learn from one another.

The precepts are also discussed at the beginning of a multiday silent residential meditation retreat, to create a safe environment in which to practice. We also discuss them, and are invited to honor them, at the beginning of MBSR teacher trainings. Following the "Principals and Standards" for teachers set forth by the UMASS Center for Mindfulness and published on the UMASS CFM website, we are asked to have a committed personal daily practice and residential retreat practice, which means we will each practice with the precepts in our own way.

My friend and senior Dharma teacher Larry Yang says, "In order to have a heart that is truly free, it must rest on a foundation of ethical conduct." He is the kind of teacher who says this not from some sort of moral high ground, although he is one of the most ethical people I have ever met, but rather from his own experiential learning, and with great compassion for how all of us humans get off course.

As with other Buddhist teachings, the intention is to practice in the spirit of compassion rather than judgment—a spirit
that creates a deep resonance of truth that we can feel in our
whole being. In chapter 8, when we come to discuss Wise
Action and Wise Livelihood, I will say more about this. For
now, here is some of what I have learned: When I have engaged
in any unskillful conduct, such as losing my temper, speaking
dishonestly, harming someone, or doing anything else outside
my values and ethics, and then I sit to meditate, awareness of
that unskillful conduct is likely going to come up and cause
great discomfort. Sitting with awareness in silence and stillness
is a great ethics teacher. I feel the effects and am much more
likely to address my behavior, to make amends for it, and *learn*
from it. Sitting helps me keep the commitment I've made to
live in accord with the precepts, because it hurts so much when
I don't, and I see how it hurts others.

The teachers I have had the privilege to train with emphasize that the precepts are not ways to shame ourselves for our
mistakes, but rather an invitation not only to feel the pain of
getting lost in unconscious or harmful behavior, but also to feel
the peace and joy that come from lack of regret, as I mentioned
regarding Wise Effort. Dharma teacher Gil Fronsdal, who has
written some wonderful articles on ethics, uses the term
"ethical sensitivity" to describe what we are cultivating with
the precepts. Practice makes us more sensitive in a good
way—we feel more, which fosters more compassion and care
for all beings.

Living in Community—the Importance of Sangha

At this point in the class we can see how important people
have become to each other, how much their communal presence and their practice matter, how much the MBSR class is a

sangha, a community of wise and kind friends. It's a great place to practice being together in this particular way and then begin to ripple it out. After all, we are all in one big community, this human community. Wise Speech and internal and external mindfulness help us create a more peaceful world, one wise word at a time.

Chapter 7

THE DHARMA OF THE
DAYLONG RETREAT: Exploring
Our Hindrances as Teachings

It's early Saturday morning, the start of the all-day retreat for the MBSR class. We've packed our lunches and put some extra yoga mats and blankets in the car. Some alumni from previous classes will be joining us and it is always a joy to see them. Hugh's class is joining also, so it promises to be a large group. While we have conducted many of these retreats, there is always that sense of not knowing; each one is unique.

The focus of this day is extending practice into seven hours, flowing seamlessly from one practice to another as well as weaving or "establishing" mindfulness in all the informal, potentially wakeful moments between formal practices. It's an opportunity to extend moment-to-moment presence in a container of silence, with plenty of support so we can have a sense of what it feels like when we are awake and aware in greater swaths of daily life.

Generally the daylong retreat in MBSR is offered after class 5 or 6. By this point in the program, most folks have developed a fairly regular meditation and yoga practice for forty-five minutes to an hour a day. They have begun to weave mindfulness into many areas of their lives in less formal, very valuable ways. What they might not have experienced is six straight hours of silence, as well as this longer continuity of practice.

We don't begin in silence; we greet each other and go over the general structure of the day. No big surprises—sitting meditation, walking meditation, body scan, yoga, repeat…Silent lunch or eating meditation, followed by, yep, you guessed it, more practice. *And* we're invited to refrain from speaking, reading, writing, or even from making much eye contact. This is how we define silence.

We set the stage for the day with some guidelines about maintaining silence and the benefits of the continuity of practice. Hugh says, "Today we have the opportunity to experience silence, which in our current culture, where we are bombarded with input and noise, is actually quite rare. This permits us to be together in a way that allows us to hear ourselves and see ourselves in a manner we might not have experienced before, that is, without talking or having to process much external information. When we set aside this quiet time, we get to 'pop the hood on our lives' and see some interesting things about how we operate. Take good care of yourselves and we'll see what happens!" What Hugh is pointing to is that what shows up on retreat can be seen as a microcosm of our lives. For example, as Nikki found out in class 2, her impatience with the body scan turned out to be her general approach to, in her words, "only everything!"

The practice of silence is a foundation of retreats and monastic or religious life dating back thousands of years. It supports meditation practice in several ways, probably many more than I can actually list. But here is what I know from my experience and my teachers.

Being in the Quiet—What It Teaches Us

Our days are filled with input, now more than ever, depending on how plugged in we are. Everything we take in has to be processed by the mind and heart in some way. If we have not had any quiet time to let all the events and pieces of data from the day digest, it can only happen when we are trying to sleep (which is one reason many of us have trouble sleeping). If you check your email or texts before you meditate, the meditation might help that activity of mind and body to settle a little bit. However, it's more likely that you'll spend a lot of the time processing all that input. And then off you go again to fill back up!

On retreat, since we don't add anything, we have the opportunity to begin to empty out. What's there under or outside all the doing? And who are we without the doing and the talking? This is what we'll explore in this chapter, but this is something you need to experience for yourself, not just read about. If you've taken MBSR and done the all-day retreat, or have sat a longer retreat somewhere else, you may have some sense of what that is for you. Take a moment and see if you can put it into words; or simply evoke the feeling. If you have not taken part in such retreats, I invite you to find a time and place to experience it.

Rather than follow the students through the retreat, I thought I would instead focus on the benefits of silent retreats as well as the challenges that they present—challenges which are in themselves teachings, as I hope you will see. I also intend to use this time to explore some key teachings within the Fourth Foundation of Mindfulness—Mindfulness of Dharmas, which will include the Five Hindrances and the Three Characteristics of Existence. So read on! It is my hope that this chapter will inspire you to find time for such daylong (or longer!) retreats and to learn a bit about how to work with what can arise.

The Five Hindrances—or Are They Guides?

During the Buddha's long sit before his awakening, he ran into various obstacles to his practice, and like everything he observed about the human condition, he taught about them! He named them as a group the Five Hindrances. Specifically, they are:

- Restlessness or Worry

- Sensual Desire or Craving

- Anger or Ill Will

- Sloth or Torpor

- Doubt

We'll go through them one by one. But let's get a little background first.

In the Fourth Foundation of Mindfulness, Mindfulness of Dharmas, the Buddha, in his usual frank, matter-of-fact, and compassionate way, simply put it out there: Along the way to awakening, and in our daily practice, there are going to be difficulties and challenges. I appreciate the fact that he includes them in the Fourth Foundation of Mindfulness so that we can see these challenges as *part* of the path to freedom, an actual doorway to freedom, not an impassable wall. The difficulties we experience may actually contain the entry point to freedom if we are conscious of them and work wisely with them.

The Buddha's experience is an example of what I mean. During the night of his awakening it is said that he was assailed by a demon named Mara, which my Zen teacher Tenshin Roshi says we can view as part of the Buddha's own psyche. Mara tried various ways to shake the Buddha off his seat, using temptations, offering him his beautiful daughters and all kind of luxuries. He also tried to frighten the Buddha with armies of warriors and terrible storms.

How did the Buddha respond? Well, he didn't succumb to temptation and run away, or we wouldn't be practicing today! What he did is in the spirit of our whole approach in MBSR.

He turned toward Mara and clearly and firmly said, "I see you, Mara." After he repeatedly did this, Mara finally left. Let's see how we too can name our own versions of Mara.

Making a Friend of Restlessness— How We Work with Worry

I did not include this in my bio, but I do consider myself to be one of the world's leading experts on the hindrance of restlessness and worry. Why? Well, I began my practice and my life with a very busy, anxious mind and a restless, energetic body. You might have already figured this out, but I did not come to the practice of mindfulness and Zen because I was a naturally mellow person. In fact, it sometimes makes me smile when folks who are restless like me say, "I don't think I can meditate because I am so anxious and I have such a busy mind, I couldn't possibly sit still and quiet my thoughts." Very like people who say, "I can't do yoga because I am not flexible." Hello! Aren't we the ones who need it the most? I'm just saying...

As for me, I would sit at home on my cushion, flooded with thoughts and a desire to hop up and check my then-snail mail, wash the dishes, or go for a walk. Sitting still was pretty excruciating. How or why I stuck with it is a bit of a mystery, except that I knew deep down that my frantic activity wasn't actually getting me where I wanted to go. It wasn't offering me the peace and relief I desperately needed. When I brought this restlessness to a meditation teacher, I was invited to bring curiosity to it.

She said, "Well, that sounds pretty normal. Why don't you try practicing *with* it rather than against it? See if you can find that restlessness in your body, the actual sensations. Notice if there is a particular pattern to the thought stream. For example, many people go constantly into the future, turning restlessness into worry."

"Yep, that's me," I said, "Always going to the future and worrying about it."

"See if you can find anything under that pull toward the future. For myself, I found it had to do with the very natural desire for safety. Go try sitting with it and tell me what you find. Then you might check in with this agitation and ask, is there anything familiar about this?"

I wasn't happy about her suggestion. On top of my busy mind and squirmy body, I had a judgment about them, which only escalated the feelings. I was restless about my restlessness. However, I trusted this teacher, so the next time I sat I tried to be curious about this feeling.

Here's what I experienced: *Hmmm, lots of thoughts going to the future, to worrying about the future.* I stopped focusing on the content or judging my thoughts. I simply noted, *Wow, busy mind.* Then on to the body: *Hmmm, lots of energy in my body, I want to move.* I continued to sit still, bringing more and more curiosity to what I was feeling, and ever so subtly and slowly my experience began to change. The part of me that was curious about the restlessness wasn't actually restless. And little by little the interest in my experience, without judgment, began to move into the foreground, and I became quieter, calmer, and stiller. Perhaps this was my way of saying, "I see you, Mara."

Did this happen in one sitting? No! But that is what makes me one of the world's leading experts on the subject. I stayed with it, really studied it until I knew it very well, and even became a little friendly with it. I remember vividly one day on retreat exploring my agitated body and mind when all of the sudden I saw something new. I realized that this feeling was deeply familiar. And I don't mean just in my meditation practice, but this feeling was the energy that drove me a great deal of the time.

I saw in this particular sitting period that what I was experiencing was my continual drive to outrun my suffering with near-constant activity, as well as the need to prove my worth, and to feel safe in an unpredictable world by trying to plan everything. The exploration of my experience in sitting led to an insight into one of the fundamental driving forces of my life. I felt tears roll down my face as I saw it and felt some sense of compassion for my busy self: *She just wants to be seen, to feel worthy, and to be safe.*

My relationship with restlessness has never been the same, and in fact I don't experience it much while sitting, though it's still likely to crop up in my everyday life (which remains a work in progress).

Seeing Is the Doorway in the Wall

Even though we might not explicitly teach the hindrances in MBSR, things like restlessness, sleepiness, irritation, doubt, and desire for something else to be happening will definitely show up. In the previous weeks, before the retreat, we've been practicing ways to "name Mara" and develop curiosity, but this is a longer stretch. So during the retreat when I look around and see folks wiggling, sighing, maybe even looking around the room or at their watches, I might just drop into the meditation guidance something like: "If you notice that you are feeling impatient and restless, see if you can bring curiosity to the feeling that is present right now. Maybe it's the urge to move, to leave, or a thought like *When is this going to be over?*—which, by the way, is just another thought. See if you can return aware-ness to the breath or hearing." Sometimes I might see a little smile or a settling, but sometimes it's just wiggle, wiggle, wiggle till the end. If this is something that comes up for you, try bringing curiosity to the sensations, thoughts, and feelings of your own agitation and see what happens.

"Ride the Wave of the Crave"—
Working with Craving and Desire

High on the list of the hindrances is sensual desire or craving. Let me just remind you that this also happens to be, according to the Buddha's careful examination of his own life, the cause of suffering! So we might want to pay attention to this. Craving as the cause of our suffering, you may recall, is named as the Second Noble Truth.

So how does this desire to have what we want show up, particularly on retreat? Over the years of teaching, one thing I have found out is that you will never get the room temperature right for everyone. At the beginning of the day I might have three people come up and ask for the temperature to be lowered and three other people already putting on sweaters and shawls. One way to work from the teaching perspective—and of course I need the reminder too—is to simply address it up front. As the group settles in, I simply name this fact. The room will not be the "right temperature" for everyone. And even if we get it right for a minute, it will change, the room and our body temperature. So what to do?

On a practical level, I invite people to wear layers. Then I assure them that each practice period will be between thirty and forty-five minutes and they will very likely survive. "Bring curiosity to the sensations, as we do in the body scan. See what happens if you note 'warm' or 'cold' without the word 'too' in front of it. Let the temperature become the focus of awareness and see what happens without the judgment and resistance." You might like to try this the next time you find yourself thinking about the "too" or "not enough" of anything.

While I might not be one of the world's leading experts on this topic, I do have a lot of experience because I am always colder than everyone else except maybe one person. No matter how many layers I bring, I can't always get it "just right," so I've learned to be very curious about what cold feels like, and I can tell you that that is a much more interesting and rewarding practice than sitting there saying inside my head, *It's too cold. I'm uncomfortable!* In addition to the fact that it adds the second arrow of suffering we spoke about in chapter 2, it also makes me quite self-centered. It's all about me. However, when I realize I'm part of a community and we're all facing some form of discomfort, needing to have my craving for warmth satisfied loosens its grip.

You can try this with other things as well. Rather than give in to a desire for something, you can relate to it differently. For instance, sometimes during a sitting period of the retreat I hear a rustling sound, I look up and see that someone has taken out his protein bar or drinking water. Apparently a craving has arisen and this is one way to respond: just follow it. Familiar? How quickly do you respond to bodily cravings?

Here's another way to "ride the wave of the crave." You want a sip of water or tea during a practice period and you don't take one. You want the snack you brought and you wait until a transition time. Feeling this desire for a drink in your body, noticing the thought, *I'm so thirsty*, noting the emotional tone—perhaps longing—and then, without doing anything, see what happens. Ride the feelings of wanting and notice if it gets stronger, stays the same, fades, or even goes away.

Whatever happens, when you place the feeling and thought complex of desire front and center in your field of awareness, it's very likely you won't be so caught in it. I've worked with this a lot because I used to suffer so much from being cold, and it has truly changed my relationship to this discomfort, which then spreads to other discomforts in life as well. After all, there are zillions of times in life when I can't get the conditions just right for me. And you? How's that going for you? To quote one of my favorite *Saturday Night Live* characters, self-help guru Stuart Smalley, "It's a lot easier to put on a pair of slippers than to carpet the whole world."

Tenshin Roshi calls retreat practice "voluntary restriction." In a non-life-or-death situation, we practice learning to tolerate our desires without immediately satisfying them, when it's *voluntary*. We not only signed up to do this, we paid for it, for Pete's sake! Then, when life throws us into an involuntary situation where we can't immediately get our needs met, we've practiced, so we don't have to suffer so much.

At the beginning of the MBSR retreat I mention this, noting the fact that it's an opportunity to see how we can relate to our desires a bit differently and not be quite so driven by them—not in a spirit of rigid deprivation, but actually out of the deep wish to be free from suffering. I also add that if after three to five breaths you feel that you need to take a sip of water, or to take your sweater off, you can. You've still increased your capacity and your resilience by simply being a little curious and putting in some space between stimulus and response.

Name It to Tame It: Working with Anger

Just as the Buddha noticed (and I bet you have, too) that craving can certainly be a challenge in our practice and in our lives, so can its counterpart, aversion. Using the above example, I could quite easily go from craving warmth to being angry that it's cold, and even angry at all the warm-blooded people who aren't cold and who may even be hot while I am suffering! Just hypothetically, of course. Anger and ill will are completely natural emotions that have their uses. For example, anger can help us set boundaries or make changes we need and want to set. However, it's also important to see where anger or a long-held resentment is not serving us, and may even be harming us.

When it comes to this particular hindrance, a former student named Margaret comes to mind. She's a regular alum at retreats. Margaret is an Amazon of a woman who came to class last summer radiating anger. She argued with me about everything and confronted me about anything. The room was too light, then too dark; the body scan was a stupid practice compared to other relaxation techniques. She preferred a mantra meditation and wanted research documentation for anything I mentioned. However, something kept her coming to class and I was curious about that. Early on, I looked back at her intake forms and saw that she was there for "jaw pain." Not much information there. I had approached her a few times before and after class to see if we could connect, to see if there was anything going on under all the irritations, but she would not engage. As the all-day retreat approached, I wondered how that would go, or if she would even come. Sure enough, she was there with deep frown creases in her forehead communicating dissatisfaction from across the room.

Just before the silent mindful lunch, Hugh and I always make it clear that we are available to anyone who might need some support in working with any challenges the day may present. We position ourselves where everyone can see us.

After a few minutes, Margaret came up. "Beth, I have to go. I just can't take it today. These thoughts, they just won't let go. They go around and around."

"Of course you absolutely can do that, but do you want to sit for a minute and talk first?"

"I really don't. I just want to leave."

"Okay. I understand." I stood up and gently touched her arm. "Just one thing, Margaret. Those thoughts? They don't actually live here at the medical center. So there is a chance they might go with you."

I saw her forehead crease relax for a minute and the beginnings of a smile play around her mouth. "You're a brat, you know that?" she replied. I think she might have wanted to use another "B" word. "I'm going to stay for a little while, I think. Can I talk to you for a minute?"

I invited her to sit with me on a bench by the pond, where we could see the ducks and geese.

"I'm just so angry, and I keep thinking about what I am angry about. I can't make it go away."

I asked if she'd be willing to try something with me that might make it possible to work with the strong feeling, and she courageously agreed.

"Can you feel the anger now?" She nodded. "Does it have a physical component in your body?"

She closed her eyes for a moment. "Yes. I feel tightness in my jaw, as always, and there is a knot in my stomach."

"Okay, what about the thoughts?"

"They keep going in circles about—well, a certain situation, and I keep finding fault, blaming."

"And the emotions?"

She opened her eyes and glared at me. "I already told you I am pissed off!"

"I hear you, you're feeling angry. Is there anything else?"

Now tears. "I don't want to go there. I don't want to talk about it." I felt a wall in her and didn't want to push. I invited her to look at the ducks swimming around and focus on her breath for a few breaths. We did this together.

Then I spoke. "For the afternoon, Margaret, I'm going to give you a few options. One is: when you feel the anger and notice the thoughts, see what happens if you go through that process. Feel it in the body, notice the thought stream and see if you can kindly label the emotion, like this: 'Ah, this is anger, I know you very well.' Another option, if that doesn't feel helpful right now, is to do some extra walking meditation around the pond. See if you can make some literal and internal space around the feeling. Or you can move back and forth between the two. How does that sound?"

She looked determined. It looked like the determination of the Buddha who would not be shaken from his seat. "I'm going to try it," she replied. I felt something different in her, like a tiny crack in the door, but I was not sure.

At the end of that retreat, I remember scanning the room for Margaret, wanting to catch her before she left. I didn't need to worry. She came right over to me and, surprisingly, took my hand, pulling me to one side of the room. I looked up at her expectantly. She had clearly been crying.

"I've been so angry since my son died four years ago." She had never mentioned this before. "And then I got in a huge fight with my brother and have pretty much been stuck on that—for years! This afternoon, I tried what you said. I was really scared. It felt like if I tried to name the feeling or face it, I'd be swallowed up by a huge monster. But what happened is I stopped telling myself the story and I just cried." Then this mighty warrior of a woman leaned down and put her head on my shoulder and wept. "I can't believe I can finally feel it now. I'm glad I stayed...I think."

For the remaining classes, a transformed Margaret engaged more with the other students and at the last class, through her tears, simply repeated the words, "I love you all."

Margaret was a powerful teacher for me, and continues to inspire me to this very day.

Bobbing Heads and Tilting Bodies: Working with Torpor

In the afternoon people often experience what the Buddha called torpor, which means low energy or lethargy. I look around the room and see heads bobbing and bodies tilting as they drop from peaceful into "sleepful." This is very common on multiday retreats as well. The hindrance of torpor is sometimes known as the "noontime demon of sleepiness."

However, truth be told, sleepiness in meditation can occur at any time in practice, and this is probably one of the most common issues that come up about meditation practice right from the start. Let's face it, we get still in the body, we close the eyes, and the body and mind say, "Hey! I know this feeling, it's time to go to sleep! Thank God. I'm exhausted." And it's lights out until our body tips so much or our head jerks forward and we are rudely awakened out of our torpor.

Now, while it is true that as a culture we are extremely sleep deprived, the Buddha addressed this hindrance over 2,500 years ago, so there must be more to it than that. Your sleep habits, however, are a good place to start if this is an issue for you. Torpor gives you a chance to look at such things as overwork or overstimulation in general and to cultivate better self-care. It's a door, not a wall.

I have a confession. This is one hindrance I have not had to face, so I have to turn to the experts here. We've talked a lot about the fact that meditation is not about going off somewhere else, and that there may be things we have not seen or not wanted to see in our practice. You can try to outrun it like me, or use sense desire to distract or numb out. You can fight it like Margaret...or you can simply doze off!

How to work with it? First, set the intention, as Jon Kabat-Zinn says, to "fall awake." Remind yourself that some part of you really wants to wake up to life—which is why you are practicing in the first place. Take a posture that embodies that intention. Then when the earliest signs of sleepiness arise, bring awareness to them. See if you can catch the first sign of the attention drifting away, like a boat slipping its moorings. Notice the smallest movement of the head going forward, the body rocking, and then give yourself support! Bring energy to the spine, opening the eyes slightly, focusing more on the inhalation. The noticing of sleepiness is not sleepy (sound familiar?). The awareness is itself an alerting mechanism and can wake you up. As with everything, we don't need to fight it or judge it, we can learn about our lives from it.

After I've offered suggestions on working with sleepiness to students, I've heard them come back and say, "I'm seeing how this same pattern shows up in my life; how I check out when things get tough. And where I 'go to sleep' to difficulties." This kind of insight is something to celebrate. Go through the door, even just a peek will do, see what's there. Report back. Repeat.

Maybe I Should Try Belly Dancing: Working with Doubt

Of all the hindrances, doubt is said to have the potential for being the greatest obstacle. If we are so unsure about the practice, or our ability to do it, that we are constantly second-guessing ourselves, it's hard to see the fruits of regular committed practice. So it may become a self-fulfilling prophecy. If we can't commit to "just doing it" and learning from whatever arises, it's quite difficult to develop a practice with the patience and persistence required for this particular path to freedom.

There are two main ways doubt shows up. One is that we doubt ourselves, our own capacity to practice, especially for an extended period of time. At the beginning of the retreat, or even the week before, this may sound like something Zach said prior to the all-day: "I don't think I can do this for seven hours." Or Eileen: "I've never been quiet for that long, it sounds too hard, I'm not the kind of person who does that." If you find yourself thinking this way, a wise response might be, "Would you be willing to try it, and simply take it one moment at a time? You don't have to bite off the whole thing at once." Another reminder is that while you may think it's going to be a certain way, the truth is that you don't know. Even I who am leading it don't know.

The other aspect of doubt is to doubt the validity of the path, the practice, or the teachings. Sometimes when people face a retreat, they might be assailed by thoughts of the many other things they could do with their time. Or they might suspect that this practice simply isn't the right one for them, and they can't see the purpose of it. I once had a woman approach me during a multiday silent retreat and say, "I thought I wanted to do mindfulness, but I think I'm going to try belly dancing. I'd prefer practicing with the movement." And then she left. Perhaps dancing and movement *are* best for her, who am I to say? However, she didn't get to find out what happens when you don't leave, and as we've seen from the examples above, there's a great deal to be learned from staying.

When the Buddha sat under that tree determined to awaken, unshaken by all the temptations of Mara, he too ultimately had to face doubt. When Mara saw that none of his other tactics were working, he asked, "Who do you think you are to awaken? Who will be your witness?"

The Buddha simply extended his hand down and touched the earth, saying, "The earth is my witness." Many depictions of the Buddha show him with the fingertips of one hand on the earth. This symbol of unshakeable commitment has been profoundly comforting to me and countless others over the years. And when doubt comes, I often take my hand and touch the earth.

Like the other hindrances, doubt will surely visit you at some time or another. When it does, you can, first, name it, investigate it through seeing the body sensations, seeing the thought as a thought, and seeing the emotional flavor. Then you can touch the earth, in your own way, touching something inside of you or around you that is steady and faithful to your commitment to be free and to contribute to the freedom of others.

Our Participant Buddhas Touch the Earth

Throughout the daylong retreat the participants have held their seats and touched the earth in their own ways. How do I know that? Primarily because they came and they stayed! Here are some of their reflections to hopefully inspire you:

Said Debbie, "In the morning I was so agitated I kind of wanted to leave, but then in the walking meditation something in me settled. For the rest of the day I felt pretty peaceful, except the parts where I just went to sleep. I really appreciated the chance to put all of this together and find out that, first of all, I could do it! I didn't think I could. The silence spoke to me and I think I want more of it. My friends and family took bets that I couldn't be silent for a whole day. I'm an extrovert who talks all the time. And you know what? I really liked the silence!"

"I'm someone who always keeps her commitments," Nikki says. "What's hard about that is that I also have a tendency to overcommit, and then I get resentful with myself and the other person. I really wanted to come today, so I backed out of something I had committed to. That's not me, but I did it anyway, this was so important to me." She is tearing up. "I really loved the day, even though parts of it were hard and I wanted to run out the door. I feel a deep peace I haven't felt since maybe before medical school ten years ago."

"Perhaps Nikki," I say, "you *are* still committed. Is it possible that you are committing to something else? Something inside you rather than outside you?" She nods slightly, looking down and wiping away the tears.

The usually quiet and self-contained businessman Peter says, "The mindful lunch was a true luxury, which surprised me. I had quite a moment with my tangerine. I've never seen how exquisite they are, and the taste was almost overwhelming. And so much goes into that small tasty fruit, it's made up of the air, water, the sun, and the earth—like the raisin! I even lay on my back on the grass and watched the clouds. I haven't done that since I was a kid."

"Right now," says Zach, "I feel really good and I'm glad I am here, but I sure had moments where I wanted to check my phone, and get outta here. I felt like I didn't see the point. I'm still not 100 percent sure this is the right thing for me, but I can't deny how I feel at this moment, which is truly peaceful."

Each person has courageously said, "I see you, Mara, I see you," and then touched the earth. As Yogi Berra said, "You can see a lot just by looking." I might just add: and by staying.

The Three Characteristics of Existence: Impermanence, Suffering, and Non-Self

An additional opportunity we have on retreat is to see into, and better yet experience, another fundamental Buddhist teaching on the nature of being human. This teaching is called the Three Characteristics of Existence, which are Impermanence, Suffering, and Non-Self. Let's look at the experience of the retreat students with the Three Characteristics.

Impermanence and Suffering

With sustained mindful awareness we're seeing that things change, that they are impermanent. People reported, "The morning was like this, and then the afternoon was like that," that at one point they were "agitated," and then they were "peaceful," and then they were "tired," and so on. In previous chapters you've seen examples of impermanence with non-threatening sensations like an itch coming and going, and more challenging ones like pain and strong emotions. The Buddha is inviting us to a deeper awareness of impermanence, and that is what Norma and Alan are working with, the realization that we and those we love will die. How can this lead to less suffering?

This awareness for Norma and Alan has led to important choices. Knowing that time is limited, they're doing what they truly want to do and what has meaning for them. What if we lived like that, if not all the time, then more of the time? The Buddha recommended that we acknowledge on a daily basis that we are "of the nature to grow old, to become ill, and to die." In our culture, this would be an outrageous suggestion. We're running madly to get away from these realities, often trying extreme health regimes and products to achieve some kind of eternal youthful immortality. Since this ultimately won't work, why not try going the other way?

In the last few years several of my close friends about my age have died. Somehow this was different for me than the death of my parents, who lived into their early eighties. As each friend was diagnosed and went through treatment, I found I began to seriously reorder my priorities, so I could spend as much time with them as possible. This meant shifting my orientation from work, on which I had become very focused, to meaningful time with my loved ones. And even though some of that time was spent in hospitals, or at their bedside while they were dying, there was a deep sense of meaning and peace that came from the connection and from the preciousness of each moment, knowing it could be the last. We even laughed our heads off at times. And watching someone you love take their last breath changes the relationship with watching one's own breath. At least that is how it is for me. Please know I am not saying that awareness of impermanence takes away our grief or rage at loss. It doesn't. But it may transform it and it may hold us while we go through it.

I have already written a lot in previous chapters about the second Characteristic of Existence, *dukkha* or suffering. The type of *dukkha* the Buddha is pointing to here is the particular suffering that comes when we look for lasting peace, happiness, and security in things that are in fact impermanent. And that, my friends, is everything.

Who Am I Really? The Teaching on Non-Self

Many folks, including our class participants here, start a retreat with concrete ideas about who they are that are a carryover from their perception of themselves in their life in general. Eileen thinks she is someone who "always talks," Nikki believes she is someone who "never breaks a commitment," Zach has the idea that he is someone who doesn't spend a day doing nothing. Each one has an idea of who they are all the time, but as the retreat unfolds they actually didn't do what they supposedly always do (or did do what they supposedly never do). So who are they now?

When people come to MBSR they may have found themselves very identified with their illness, perceiving themselves as "a cancer patient" rather than as a mom, a social worker, a woman, a friend, a sister, as a playful, crazy, smart human being who happens to have cancer right now. It can also work with things we feel great about: "I am a successful business person." So what happens to "you" when you fail? Are you still you? "I am a nice person." So what happens when you give someone the finger in traffic? Are you still you?

What if you think, "I am a mindfulness practitioner," and then drive off with your coffee cup on the roof of your car or lose your keys right before you have to be somewhere? Do you then have to use your practice against whom and what you call yourself? I'm just asking.

Here is a line of inquiry to explore. If you experience anger frequently or occasionally, does that make you "an angry person"? How does it feel to say I *am* angry versus I *feel* angry? Your feelings don't need to define you, because you are still whole and you still have kindness, humor, wisdom, and humanity, even when you feel horribly sad. Your goodness does not go away when you're upset, any more than the sun disappears when it is cloudy and we can't see it.

My takeaway? We're verbs, not nouns.

In the teaching on non-self, please understand that the Buddha didn't teach that there is no self. What he actually said was, "If you look for a self, you will not find it." Meaning, in part, that if you look for a constant, "always like this" self you won't find it—when you are really curious and paying attention. We've seen the kind of suffering Brian experienced around the idea that he was "always there for everyone," and then became dependent on his family for everything. As he has slowly accepted his new role and even found that his family likes helping him, he is suffering less. The practice of non-self is a practice of investigation, a practice that leads to seeing this changing nature of everything, including ourselves, and how this insight may reduce our suffering. It is not, I repeat not, about getting rid of anything. Like all our practices and realizations, it is about seeing into the nature of things. When we look deeply, who—and more importantly, what—are we?

If you look really closely, you may find that how you define yourself is not as fixed and constant as you think, and that the story of "me" or "you" may in fact be simply a story. It's true that I have a name someone gave me, a birthplace, a gender, a skin color, and a history. But that history and all those other things may be spun in any number of ways. I have certain preferences and things I absolutely don't like. But is that "me"?

So just take a look and see if that self is as real and fixed as you thought. See if your tension and suffering decrease a little bit if you hold the story more loosely and fluidly.

Vietnamese Zen master Thich Nhat Hanh says it this way. He will often hold up a flower and say, "This flower is made of nonflower elements, it's got the sun, the earth, the rain and sky in it." (He does this with a piece of paper, too.) "And you too are made of non-self elements." Physics would tell us that what looks like matter made of atoms is really mostly space.

Now, having a "functional self," as Jack Kornfield calls it, can also be really useful, and quite wonderful if we know and use it wisely. When I practice medicine, I wear a white coat and a stethoscope. I carry other instruments and a prescription pad; these are the tools of my trade and they inspire clarity and confidence in my patients. It's also practical! At the end of the day, however, I get to (and need to) put them down. I've found many times over thirty years that when I carry that caregiver role around with me too much, I suffer a lot and so does my family. And it goes both ways, so if you see me in Starbucks, please don't show me your rash. (Yes, this happens.) Tenshin Roshi wears robes in the zendo, but in town he wears jeans and says, "I'm a dad who coaches soccer."

We've both found, as many people have, that it's painful to be confined to a role, whether it is seen as positive or negative. The Buddha's invitation to simply take a look at what I call "me" has helped me with this type of suffering tremendously. See what is true for you.

Chapter 8

THE DHARMA OF ACTION AND LIVELIHOOD: Working with Our Ethical Compass

Among my many patients today was the lovely Graciella, as gracious as her name. She's a waitress at the steak house connected to one of the local casinos. Graciella is on her feet all day, which is hard on her arthritic knees. I don't have an easy answer for her. We'd both like her to lose weight. Physical therapy might help, and some supplements, but she has a very full schedule. It's hard for her to get off work, and there is always someone in her extended family who needs her care. So while it is not ideal, I give her a cortisone shot in the left knee. We can only do these every four months, but it's been more than that since the last one. It gives her lots of relief. This is one of those areas where I feel the temporary benefit outweighs the risk *for now.* But over time this will change and we'll have to find another solution.

I mentioned in chapter 6 that I had trained in martial arts. Part of what I studied was "grappling," which is based on jujitsu and involves a lot of rolling around on the floor gripping your opponent and trying not to get choked. Why am I telling you this? In this chapter we're going to focus on what I'll call "engaged mindfulness": bringing awareness into all aspects of our lives—family, work, and society at large. In other words, practicing mindfulness as a path to living in connection with our values, with our ethics, and with the whole planet. We looked at this in chapter 6 as we explored one of the ethical factors of the Eightfold Path—Wise Speech. One might say that engaged mindfulness is, in part, about doing the right thing in the moment and seeing the long-term ramifications. It's a practice of looking deeply at ways in which we may live while causing as little harm and as much good as possible. And the truth is, the word "grappling" keeps coming up for me as I reflect on this. As I grapple with ethics in my profession these days, and as I am now grappling with how to write about this part of the path, I remember what physical grappling felt like in my body in those earlier days. And you know what? When it comes to ethics, I believe we're supposed to grapple. It's not meant to be easy, and that's okay, because we are strong and it's worth it.

This chapter also gives us a chance to circle back to the refrain from the teaching on the Four Foundations of Mindfulness, where the Buddha asks us to "contemplate the field of awareness, both internally and externally." In this section we're shining the light on the "external" contemplation. This, of course, cannot be truly separated from what is going on internally, but we'll simply focus on the external aspect a bit more here.

As we explore this here, you'll note that I am using the words "values" and "ethics." I asked long-time educator Jo Marie ("Joey") Taylor to help clarify the difference between what is meant by these two terms. As someone who spent thirty-two years working in inner city schools with young children, she says, "Values are formed as we grow developmentally. They become part of our character, and are dear to our heart, and can be quite individual to ourselves. While they are of course informed by our tribe and our conditioning, they are intrinsic and personal. Ethics seem to me slightly further out, developing more externally in terms of how we interface with the world. In kindergarten I introduce them in terms of how we're going to get along together peacefully and learn together effectively if we obey certain guidelines. However, rather than preaching and punishing, I try to show the kids, through real-time examples, how destructive it can be when we don't follow them, and how good it feels when we live together this way." Joey's words and experience rang true for me, so when I use these terms, going forward, this is what I'm working with.

With regard to my physician assistant career, in terms of mindfulness, ethics, values, and my work, on the surface it might seem straightforward—practicing medicine is a valuable way to support oneself: caring for others, with the intention to enhance the well-being of people through education, diagnosis, and treatment. When I started out, it felt that way to me. But I was young and things have changed. In medicine we take an oath to "First, do no harm." But doing no harm is actually not so easy or clear. The example with Graciella is a case in point. The steroid shot over the long haul is not good for the joint, but in the short term and used judiciously, it will probably be okay, and it allows her to function, given the realities of her particular life circumstances. It's a complex system and there are many things that influence our decisions—insurance companies, pharmaceutical companies, and massive advertising campaigns, to name a few. Every medication we prescribe has side effects, every procedure we do has risks. My colleagues and I are continuously weighing the risk/benefit ratio. Even when I feel I have made a fairly good decision, the insurance company or the patient may not agree with me. Then I have to reassess and often compromise.

I'd love to tell you that at the end of the day I have done more good than harm, but I can't really know. What I can tell you is that my intention is to be beneficial and to continue to care and continue to grapple. Which means I have to be willing to be really uncomfortable, like in my martial arts days, when I would come home covered with bruises. I know that I want to approach my work with an open heart and with integrity. This is what I want. I don't do it perfectly by a long shot, but I am committed to trying to stay awake to the whole messy thing.

Graciella is grappling with the work she does, too. The casino provides a lot of jobs in our community, but she doesn't feel good about gambling. She knows many of her regular customers by name, knows their families, too. Today she told me, "Poor Mr. Andrews lost so much money, he was so upset. But I know he'll go back and try again. I just hate it."

I understand. I deal with many people who are addicted to a variety of things, including gambling. It is indeed painful to watch. In my case I say no a lot to demands for Vicodin and Oxycodone. Some patients leave angry and dissatisfied, and I feel that way, too. Here again, there is no easy answer, but my intention to practice mindfully wraps itself around me and holds me through the storm. Like living on the mountain, the weather may be stormy, but underneath I can find some stillness. Something solid on which I can rest.

While I am grappling, I actively use what I've learned from MBSR and my Buddhist practice. I use the awareness of breathing and of the body to help clarify my decision making. For example, when I'm stressed, I focus on my breath until the blood flow gets back to the prefrontal cortex. When I am frustrated, I connect to my heart, to my good-will intentions. I'm aware of the Noble Truth of Suffering, and how I may make it worse by craving for things to be done my way, the "right" way. I know only too well the pain of allowing my agenda to occlude my vision of the person right in front of me, who deserves my attention right now. I apply Wise View, Wise Intention, Wise Effort, and Wise Speech. I practice in this way because I really need this stuff! It is really painful when I get off track, so I try not to go numb or go to sleep. Also, practicing in this way helps me be a better health care provider and to be more compassionate to my patients. And even if I am unable to get others to lower their blood pressure by meditating, at least I can try it myself.

Ethics in the Classroom

In the MBSR classroom I am very attentive to the practice of "engaged or external mindfulness," connecting consciously to my ethics and values as MBSR teachers around the globe do. This is not personal to me, mind you; it is integral to the practice and the program. For example, in MBSR, while I don't prescribe medication which may have side effects, I also try not to prescribe anything else, such as my agenda. Yes, I sometimes have one, that's the truth: I want people to get better. But over time I have learned that I don't know what "better" is for each individual. I'm not even sure what it is for me. I try to notice when I am getting attached to a certain outcome, or am upset when someone is struggling. When I notice that, I turn my attention inward and do my own work of practice.

What are some specific ways to stay connected to my ethics and values? I work closely with the UMASS Center for Mindfulness Standards of Practice. I reflect on the precepts regularly at the Zen center and at home, and most importantly, *I don't do it alone.* If I have a student who pushes my buttons or who wants to be my BFF, I talk about it with someone. We work it through. And I use the precepts as a framework: Am I being truthful? With them and myself? Am I practicing harmlessness? Can I find compassion? Am I clear about not taking what is not offered? Clear with sexual boundaries? Am I intoxicated in some way—for me, not with substances, but perhaps with my ideas?

Experience has shown me that I am much less likely to get lost in craving, in justification, or in rationalization, as we all do, if I am in close contact with a teacher, a mentor, or a group of peers, friends, and colleagues—which I am. People know what I am up to. I am quick to call on a therapist when I need to. We need each other to stay connected to ourselves. When I work with new teachers, one of the first things we talk about is the importance of having a personal practice which includes all of the above. Not just sitting, but Sangha—connection to wise people to whom we are accountable, with whom we can honestly share our struggles. I strongly say, "We cannot do this alone!"

A Hand on the Tiller

As I drive to the medical center for class 7 of the MBSR class, I am looking forward to hearing about the effects of the retreat. Entering the room, I see a small crowd of people around Norma and Alan, and I go over to welcome them back. I can see Alan has lost some weight, but also that he is glowing. They are both smiling as they tell Joe, Renée, and Eileen about the car show. I want to hear it all, but I need to gather us together.

The theme of class 7 is mindfulness in daily life, including looking at how and what we consume—what we take in and what we leave out. In other words, bringing awareness to the wide circle of our life and our society. It will be interesting to see how the longer period of practice on Saturday informed people's lives and actions. I ask for reflections from the week. "What did you notice after the retreat? How is your practice going? What is happening in your life?"

"We were up north at the car show, as you know," Alan says. "It was really great to see a lot of old friends, and my car placed third! It was an important trip, and I thoroughly enjoyed it. If we weren't in this class, I'm not sure I would have made it a priority. I don't think I would have even considered it. But I could feel that it would be meaningful, and it was. It's my last car show and I'm glad I didn't miss it."

"And we did our body scans every day!" Norma chimes in. I noticed a poignant tender expression on her face as Alan was sharing.

I feel a surge of both happiness and sorrow, and tears spring to my eyes as I listen to them and see them, taking in this important message to all of us with my entire being. I ride the wave of emotions for a moment and see that other people are leaning in toward them, and a few of them have tears sparkling in their eyes, too. One of them is Joe.

"Well, you may recall, I had a minor love affair with my tangerine at the silent lunch on Saturday," Peter says, smiling. "I mean really! The exquisite intricacies of the sections and the flavor, wow! To my surprise, when I walked through the door at home, my daughter was practicing the piano, and I saw her the same way. It stopped me in my tracks. She is so beautiful. And the sounds of the piano—I don't know that I have truly taken her in, in so long, maybe…" he looks down, choking up a bit, "not since she was a baby. She's thirteen now. The day, and the way I felt and still feel, allowed me to feel the contrast to how I've been living and feeling. So…tight. I've been con-sumed by work. I forgot the other important things. It carried over into dinner, I looked at my family, I tasted the lasagna, I felt so grateful to my wife."

We all breathe with him in silence for a moment, as if we too were savoring this moment with his family.

"Is there more, Peter?" I ask. I have a feeling there's some-thing with his work.

"When I started the class, I know I just said I was here for work stress. It's only recently that I realize how bad things really are there and how angry and actually hurt I feel about some of the behavior in the organization. There are some questionable issues and practices, and I've suppressed my opinion. I know something has to change. I have to change."

"Thank you, Peter. It takes a lot of courage to face these kinds of complicated issues. Is there anything you're learning here that may help you make the changes you want to make?"

"Absolutely. I have been really committed to the body scan, and this connection with my body has become like the rudder on a sailboat for me. When you sail you have to be aware of the wind and the weather, notice the direction and tautness of the sails. But you also have to have your hand on the tiller and be aware of the rudder deep below the surface of the water. You have to know what direction you're going in and have some flexibility as well. The whole process is this interaction between the wind, the weather, the sails, and the rudder. I feel like up until recently my attention was almost completely on the wind and the sails, the pressures and agendas of other people and the organization at large. I wasn't very connected to the tiller and the rudder. I wouldn't say I took my hand off altogether, but I wasn't very in touch with it. The rudder here is my personal values, my internal guidance system. This slowing down we do here, the quietness, this getting in touch with what things literally feel like in my body, has gotten my hand more firmly on the tiller. Of course I still have to interplay with the wind and the weather, but I am connected to something deeper. That was missing. Now I can feel and see the beauty of my family, and I can feel the pain of the situation at work. These things also guide me and move me to make change. Does that answer your question?"

I am covered with goose bumps. Peter has expressed so beautifully a vitally important reason to practice. Over the years, I have given many PowerPoint lectures about the research on the benefits of mindfulness at medical conferences. I can give you loads of reasons to meditate, from the cellular level to the behavior-change level. But what I really want to say is this—having a practice is a good way to make sure you are living *your* life, your own life, the one that aligns with your deepest values, rather than the one that happens, to use Peter's analogy, when we are blown by the winds without our hand on the tiller.

To my mind, the best part about his realization, his experience, is that he came to it on his own and now it is fully his. And as he told it, the class was riveted, you should have seen their faces, their rapt attention. He is demonstrating how he is reconnecting to his deepest, truest values through his practice, and serving as an example to the rest of us.

Nikki raises her hand. "Thank you, Peter, that is so helpful! Beth, I thought a lot about the question you asked me at the retreat, when I felt badly about breaking a commitment. You asked if maybe I was still committed, but to something else. Listening to Peter, I realize that I too have been blown around a lot by the wind. I think now I'm more committed to the rudder. Or at least I want to be. That is my intention. It's so easy to lose sight of why I went into medicine in the first place." She smiles at him. "I think my choice to come on Saturday was like putting my hand on the tiller."

"Just one quick thing," says Raúl. "Oh, sorry, two. We noticed how much less we're spending at Costco! It just happened, I mean our bill is hundreds of dollars less. Also, my Little League team is doing great. They're really getting into this mindfulness thing!"

In class 7 we often explore together the impact of what we are taking in through media and technology, through what we eat and what we buy. However, the students are clearly doing the laboratory work in their lives and presenting their findings. There is certainly no need here for me to say much about mindfulness in daily life, nothing to add.

Wise Doing Through Non-Doing

As we move into the way the Buddha taught about the ethical aspects of the Eightfold Path, which, in addition to Wise Speech (covered in chapter 6), are Wise Action and Wise Livelihood, we'll begin by looking at them firsthand, from the MBSR practitioner view and from our own experience. Have you ever heard someone refer to meditation practice as "navel gazing"? Or perhaps even worried yourself that taking time in silence and stillness might make you passive? It seems there is a nagging concern that we might be less engaged with life without the *seemingly* motivating energies of worry, fear, and anger. I totally get it. I've wondered myself more than a few times.

But what experience has actually shown—and by experience I do mean mine, yes, but also that of hundreds of thousands of folks, let alone thousands of years of history—is that when we quiet down, feel the body, notice the thought-feeling stream, and stop running around, we may actually encounter what is really troubling us and be moved to do something from a place of calm, connected clarity. We may be moved by compassion. We make better choices, we take more positive actions. We've seen this in the class above. Peter, Nikki, and Raúl are making important changes, or at least asking the deep questions that often lead to change, because they have allowed themselves to feel the discomfort under the disconnection. They are connecting with something deeper than the wind in the sails, and finding which way to point the boat. We may also be motivated to make change and to take wiser action out of great love. I sense that for Peter, reconnecting with the love for his family is an equally strong motivator for him to make changes that transform his feeling of discomfort and disconnection with his values at work. Similarly with Eileen, feeling her love for teaching and for children is part of her rudder as well, it has caused her to reevaluate and be more connected. Just as we feel moved to live and act wisely out of care for our families and friends, in the realm of our connection with the welfare of the earth we may conserve water or reduce our carbon footprint out of great love for the planet and all its inhabitants. Mother Teresa said, "We don't have to do great things, only small things with great love." That's the practice of Wise Action and Wise Livelihood.

Wise Action and Wise Livelihood

On the Eightfold Path we are now at the factors of Wise Action and Wise Livelihood, the classical way of saying what I have called "engaged mindfulness." Along with Wise Speech, this is where our practice informs our decisions, our words, our behavior, our actions, and our work in the world. In many ways it is a natural outgrowth of turning inward. As Peter so beautifully articulated, it seems that when we are willing to touch our experience intimately, we may become connected to our inner ethos, our moral compass.

In the classical teachings the Buddha was quite specific and clear about the practice of Wise Action and Wise Livelihood. As always, the guiding questions are: What will lead to less suffering? What might lead to more suffering? The questions here expand beyond our personal suffering and ask us to consider at the societal level: What makes for a more wholesome community? What fosters a healthier, saner society? Just as Joey asked her kindergarteners!

The Buddha zeroed in on three areas that have been identified by all other traditions as well, because they are the three areas known to cause us the most suffering. Simply put, Wise Action is actions in accord with the precepts, but in particular:

- Abstaining from taking life, while cultivating and honoring life.

- Abstaining from taking what is not given, fostering a generous heart.

- Abstaining from sensual and sexual misconduct, encouraging respectful and honest relationships.

Please refer back to chapter 6 if you'd like to revisit the precepts.

The precepts are not dictums imposed on us by an external source. They are guidelines—ways to encourage us to explore and become more conscious of our choices. For example, one of the precepts is "Do not kill." In the strictest sense, we get that killing living beings leads to suffering. It often stems from certain forms of suffering—greed, anger, and ignorance—and is itself, in fact, a form of suffering. But when people hear this guideline about refraining from killing, they often wonder: "Does this mean I should be a vegetarian? What about the ants swarming the kitchen?" Then from there, "What happens to living beings from the fossil fuels I use? Am I using them wisely?" Where I live we have a drought, so I ask myself about my water use all the time, because I know it hurts the planet if I don't. Please know I am not pushing my own agenda: these are questions that often arise in communities that practice together and discuss the precepts together, and among people from all walks of life who have their own ethos, their own traditions.

These are important questions to ask. It is vital that we ask them. Not asking them at all has led to a lot of harm. We see this reflected in a myriad of ways, from wars without end, to racially motivated killing, social injustice, and climate change. So let's at least ask, let's allow ourselves to *feel* the discomfort that killing or harming in all its many forms causes, and then be guided from there.

Obviously these are complex issues with many factors, so without oversimplifying, it simply makes sense to start with awareness. We can find out where our food comes from, where our clothing comes from. Is someone being harmed in the process? Where do we find balance? Do we speak up against injustice? Can we bring about change with our wallets? Let's ask ourselves these questions and see how we feel when we find out, and how that affects our behavior. Remember, we're grappling to find the right answers; we are invited to do rather than follow a set of external rules.

Wise Livelihood Today

When it comes to Wise Livelihood, in the context of our lives today and in the context of this book and our class, here is another place where we can practice investigation and make changes to the best of our abilities. Perhaps, like Graciella, you have a job that may not represent your deepest values—but it fits your skills, and your need to support your family. So perhaps you focus less on *what* you do than on *how* you do it. You can see that the folks in the class are doing this. Something has changed for Raúl, for Nikki, for so many of them. You don't have to quit your job and live in a monastery—you can make a "temple" in your office with compassion and awareness.

That's not to say that it's not worth looking at your options. For me, teaching MBSR and working part time as a physician assistant, though much less financially secure than many other career options, is more in alignment with my heart's calling. It's not necessarily easier; it's just a different kind of challenge that for me feels like Wise Livelihood, even if it means living with less certainty. And after all, what is really certain anyway?

The Art of Non-Harming

Non-harming is one of those "grapple" topics that depends on so many factors, including your circumstances. At our house, *sometimes* we gently escort spiders, beetles, and other creatures from the house in our "bug buggy" and place them outside. This small action, I've found, has an interesting effect on me. In the moment it takes to slow down, catch the creatures, take them outside, and watch them reorient and then move away, I am present to the life force in them, in myself, and then in everyone. It becomes a practice of interconnectedness.

On the other hand, if you have a baby and black widow spiders in your house, you might deal with them differently. So would I. Up here in the mountains a common dilemma is how we deal with rattlesnakes. In this case, again, if you have pets and children it will be different than if you don't. It's about the intention to honor life, and each person decides what that looks like, moment by moment. My friends in the military and law enforcement have a whole other set of decisions to make: it's a big grapple and they deal with it as best they can.

I recently came home to what I thought was an empty house after a long trip. Only it wasn't so empty. There was a large blue centipede, known to be poisonous, on the bedside table (who is still MIA, gulp), a baby racer snake in the bathroom, and a kitchen counter covered with ants. I dealt with each situation differently and went to bed relatively at peace. Above all it reminded me that I am not alone. I'm sharing this planet with all kinds of beings and it belongs to all of us.

On a more subtle level, if you're in a retreat and there is a talk or discussion about the precepts, or like at Yokoji Zen Mountain Center where we have a monthly day of reflection on the precepts, you might reflect on ways you kill off parts of yourself. Is there some part of yourself that you hate? What do you do when you encounter it? Do we mentally kill off someone else's opinions or feelings? This is another level of investigation worthy of our attention.

When we begin to discuss sexual conduct, we're entering an arena where simple pronouncements of right and wrong often fail us and deteriorate into taking empty moral positions. Each of us has to find our own guidance and our own way. For monks and nuns in certain communities it may mean refraining from sex completely. For lay people it is a place of practice, and a very crucial place to stay awake.

It is particularly important to stay awake to our sexual conduct when there is power discrepancy—refraining from sexual exploitation and the use of power for sexual relations when it involves minors, children, and anyone who may be vulnerable and not empowered to protect themselves. Many professions have ethical guidelines that include not having a sexual relationship with a student, client, or patient. The issues around sexual misconduct have caused an untold amount of suffering. This also ties in directly with Wise Speech—truthfulness—as well as to the precept not to harm living beings.

Just recently it came to my attention that two men in my community have had sexual relations that violate what I know to be their own value systems. In one case it was the husband of a dear friend who had an affair with a young woman while in his twenty-eighth year of marriage. In another case it was a teacher with a student. These are good, kind, well-intentioned men. What happened? Their behavior shows us what can happen when we get lost or intoxicated in sensual pleasure. And what I have noticed in both situations is that while the people most closely affected have been deeply hurt, these men are also suffering terribly. It's like they woke up out a trance and are filled with remorse and even self-loathing. They are examples of how important it is to stay awake for everyone's sake. Practice offers us this possibility, practice and the kind of connection with other people who are committed to examining their ethics and asking the hard questions. Any of us can get lost in this way, but as I said earlier, if we take refuge in our sangha it is much less likely.

In an exchange between the Buddha and his attendant Ananda, Ananda says to the Buddha, "Venerable sir, this is half of the spiritual life: good friendship, good companionship, good comradeship."

"Not so, Ananda, not so!" the Buddha replied. "This is the *entire* spiritual life. When you have a good friend, a good companion, a good comrade, it is to be expected that you will cultivate the Noble Eightfold Path."

In the context of what we are talking about, I feel I now understand this teaching in a deeper way. As I said before, and say generally to Dharma students and MBSR teacher trainees, "We can't stay on course alone." This is what this dialogue means to me. Please contemplate what it means to you.

At the Insight Community of the Desert, where I teach, we have quite a few people in recovery who attend regularly. After a talk on the importance of community, of sangha, one man shared, "We have an AA meeting here called the Cornfield Group. The couple who started it named it that because they noticed, on a cross-country road trip, that the corn in the center of the field grows the tallest. History shows that people are a lot less likely to relapse if they stay close to other recovering alcoholics."

Someone immediately asked, "How do we all get to be in the center of the field?"

"We take turns," he replied.

We can all learn from this great example, knowing that while we might not suffer from that particular addiction, we are vulnerable to craving in various ways and can get swept up in it. Here we can call on our Wise Intention, our Wise Effort, and find the foundation of renunciation and honesty.

Many years ago I had an MBSR participant, Tanya, who was a brilliant young graduate student getting her doctorate in physics. She came to MBSR with what seemed like mostly academic curiosity. She seemed to hold herself a little apart from the group and often asked questions that I couldn't fully understand. One of the habitual places I go to is, "I'm just not smart enough to help her or answer her." The wiser part of me, however, knows that mindfulness practice is not about this kind of intellectual intelligence, and I tried to just stay open to her, allowing both of us to "not know." When I did, I could see there was something she was struggling with and it wasn't something either of us could get to easily or quickly.

Finally one day Tanya asked if we could speak privately. She spoke rapidly and without interruption and I sat patiently, my confusion growing, as I looked for someplace to land, someplace to meet. I couldn't find one. After about forty minutes, she told me that she was having an affair with one of her professors. She offered a careful and possibly much-rehearsed explanation for why it was okay for both of them. I just listened. But I had a sense now of what was driving all her confusion and discomfort.

The practice and the honest sharing in class were holding up a mirror in which she had the opportunity to see her choices and the consequences of those choices more clearly. My role was to simply bear witness and to hold her feet kindly to the fire of her growing discomfort by not offering anything but my undivided nonjudgmental attention and my own clear ethics, which I showed only through my attention. I didn't ask questions or offer suggestions, because she wasn't asking me for any. My hope was that her discomfort would actually increase enough to guide her to her own wise and honest heart.

I don't know exactly what she did or what she learned, but it was a great teaching for me. I once heard Jack Kornfield say, regarding ethics, "It's pretty hard to meditate after a day of lying, cheating, and stealing." Since having an affair involves all of these, Tanya's MBSR practice was really challenging.

With Eileen, the elementary school teacher, after a few weeks of practice she knew she had to rectify things with the student she had yelled at. Peter is feeling how painful it is not to stand up for his ethics at work, and is willing to do so. In the original teaching on suffering, the Buddha spoke about the unnecessary suffering—the second arrow that leads to more suffering—and the necessary suffering that leads to less suffering. It seems that Wise Action and Wise Livelihood might come under the category of the suffering that leads to less suffering.

Back at the beginning of this book I talked about ways that mindfulness of the body may lead to an increase in our awareness of pain, and how people sometimes ask, "Why the heck would I want to do that?" I wrote about how that awareness can often lead to taking better care of the body. In that same way, the pain of the way things are often leads to the deepest social change. Dr. Martin Luther King Jr. felt the pain of racism, so he did something; Mother Teresa felt the pain of poverty, so she did something. They also shared a great love of humanity and a deep desire to care for us, and this love motivated them as well. But you don't have to be a great hero to practice wise and engaged action. All of us have this capacity, including you. You are very likely practicing it in more ways than you realize. Sometimes the pain of the reality of this life can be the impetus for Wise Action and Wise Livelihood, and sometimes it's our great love. Feeling it can be the way home to our hearts.

Chapter 9

THE DHARMA OF WISDOM:
Practice, Practice, Practice

All day I have been weaving in and out of exam rooms, seeing patients. Not just seeing, but using all my senses. Feeling for the edges of the liver with my fingertips on an abdomen, smelling the sickly sweet scent of high blood sugar, peering down ear canals and throats, and listening. I listen to patients' stories and I also place my stethoscope gently on their backs and hear the sounds of breathing, sometimes smooth and full like the wind, sometimes wheezy and tight like rusty machinery. I place the bell of the stethoscope on their chests and listen to their hearts.

Physical exam and diagnosis are mindfulness practice, concentration practice. When I teach mindfulness to medical and physician assistant students and nurses, I encourage them to look up from their computers and take in the whole person. You'd be surprised—or maybe you wouldn't—how many of my patients tell me I'm the first person who has physically examined them in this mindful, personal way in years. For me it is not only a way of gathering information, it is way of connecting and slowing down, even when I don't want to. Believe me, I want to rush ahead as much as anyone—but I feel the impulse and then I don't follow it. This takes practice. Today, with so much going on, I use my practice, my awareness, to keep me present and on track. And when I remember to do it, I find I actually enjoy myself more than when I'm distracted or rushed, and I learn a lot.

It has been a full day. My dear old friend and patient Arthur came in. So far we've managed to get him enough home health care to keep him home with his beloved pets. He is not quite as sad as last time, and when I tell him that the birdbath he gave me is being visited by a doe and her fawn in addition to the woodpeckers, he brightens considerably. Still, he is fading and his heart sounds are somewhat faint. He has the distinctive sound we hear with congestive heart failure.

I listen to the booming heart sounds of Miss Ruby, a giant of a woman, Baptist minister and leader in the African-American community here. She showers me with blessings and tells me I am in her prayers. Then I listen to the energetic heart sounds of eight-year-old Jennifer, who is getting a checkup for soccer. She's good to go.

Learning to Fish

Ahead of me lies class 8, the final class of this round of MBSR. Driving to the hospital, I reflect on this poignant time of the program, when we say goodbye and usually share much gratitude for one another. This group, like all groups, has touched and inspired me. I don't really want to say goodbye, and yet it's also good to come to the end of the cycle. When I think about my journey with this group of people, I guess you could say I've been listening to hearts here, too. We've all been listening to ourselves and one another.

Yesterday Hugh's eight-week MBSR cycle at the cancer center came to an end. When he got home, I asked, "So how was it?" He said, "I want to show you something." He dug in his backpack and pulled out a red leather box. Opening it, he revealed an exquisite gold compass with a map of the world in the background. Then he handed me a card. It said, "Thank you for showing us how to find our own way." There were a dozen signatures. What else would an MBSR teacher or any teacher want to hear?

His gift reminds me of a card I received a few years ago. On the front was a colorful woodblock print of a fisherman on a bridge. Inside it said, "Give someone a fish and you feed them for a day, teach someone to fish and you feed them for a lifetime. Thank you for teaching us to fish." I don't know how my group will feel or what they will say, but as you've seen, they have been fishing on their own for sure. I hope that your experience with your personal practice has offered you a way to work with your own compass or taken you on your very own fishing expedition, in your own way.

What Has Changed?

The classroom is buzzing with people connecting with each other as I enter. I see Brian and Zach with their heads together, talking animatedly. The class quiets a bit, but only a bit, as I take my seat—it takes several rings of the bells to get their attention. We start this evening where we began several weeks ago: on the floor with a long body scan. The room becomes settled and still and I sink into it myself. Once we are seated again, I ask, "How was that for you? Any difference from eight weeks ago?"

Nikki shares first: "I notice I am able to stay so much more with it—with the body scan—than I used to be, I don't feel *quite* as impatient, though I still notice the thought: *Oh my God, a whole other arm, really?* But it makes me smile now, and I just say to myself: *Oh yeah, another one of those thoughts*, and then I go back to the arm..." She smiles that playful smile of hers. "But seriously, this practice is helping me stay focused with my patients and my family. I notice this urge to check my phone, but I just notice it and bring my attention back to listening."

Lisette says, "I can really feel my body now. At the beginning there were a lot of parts that were kind of numb. I know this is what has changed the way I eat, and why I am losing weight. It's really uncomfortable to overeat. And healthier foods, well, they feel good afterward."

"I remember being really fearful and skeptical about the body scan," says Jean. "Because I was in so much pain." (I remember this, too!) "But sticking with this practice has really changed the way I am with myself. I'm not so afraid of feeling my body. In fact, I'm just not so afraid, period. I'm willing to stay with myself in a different way, even when I'm in pain, and that means I can stay with other challenging things in my life, and then, well, they're just another thing, not such a big deal. I actually think I'm pretty courageous." She holds her head up a little.

I reply, "I agree, Jean. From the very first time you tried the body scan you showed tremendous courage. Thank you for sharing it with us."

There are more comments about less mind wandering and less judgment when the mind does wander, and more awareness of the body, with less judgment about the body. Many people notice that they are handling things differently, seeing new options. There is also the simple truth that in eight weeks people have observed that things change. In fact, if we're paying attention, we can see that in eight minutes or eight seconds things change.

Final Steps on the Eightfold Path: Wise Mindfulness and Wise Concentration

All along we've been talking about mindfulness. In fact it is the first word in "Mindfulness-Based Stress Reduction"! Now, as we near the end of the class and the end of the Eightfold Path, we're looking at mindfulness again through the lens of the wisdom developed by the other factors. For me it raises the question, what is meant by *Wise* Mindfulness? Reflecting on the participants' comments in the context of Wise Mindfulness and Wise Concentration, it may be grounded in part in the ongoing development of the "nonjudgmental" attitude fostered and cultivated throughout the program. From my own practice and from listening to people talk about "nonjudgment" over the years, I have come to realize that there is so much packed in that seemingly simple phrase—qualities like curiosity, kindness, compassion, and patience, to name a few.

Because the Eightfold Path is a way to be free, and wisdom shines the light on this way, then wisdom means being more accepting and compassionate with ourselves and others. It includes Nikki's attitude of humor and the powerful recognition, "Oh, it's one of those thoughts" and "It's just a thought." Before, these were defining statements that ruled her life. Now she is less caught by them. Lisette's Wise Mindfulness has led to her eating more healthily. And Jean's has led to her living with less fear and more creativity.

Remember when I said the Eightfold Path wasn't linear, that it's more like a twisted rope with many strands, each strand making the whole rope stronger? Here we are nearing the end of a book about Mindfulness-Based Stress Reduction, and about the Eightfold Path in which mindfulness is front and center, and we're visiting it again—at the end. But now we've added many strands to the rope. Our mindfulness practice is now informed by reflecting on our view—awareness of the Four Noble Truths and a greater understanding of the lens we may be looking through. It has been strengthened by Wise Intention and Wise Effort, which include the strands of renunciation, good will, and compassion. And it rests firmly on our ethics: Wise Speech, Wise Action, and Wise Livelihood. Hopefully now your Wise Mindfulness goes beyond simply seeing clearly and being with what you find, and informs more of what you do and how you live with the reality of what you see and feel. The more we practice, the more it becomes our rudder and our wind.

With this understanding in the background, we can also look at what mindfulness is not. Buddhist scholar and teacher John Peacock says, "Mindfulness is not cold staring." As a meditation teacher, I find much time in class is spent guiding folks to discern the difference between critical, evaluative thinking and the present-moment awareness of Wise Mindfulness that includes kindness, openness, and curiosity. When people share their experience and it includes their struggle to pay attention and their frustration with their mind and body, these are indications that they are subtly or not so subtly *evaluating* their experience as not the right experience, rather than simply being with it and seeing it clearly, or standing near it with kindness. Now, evaluating is completely normal, we're highly conditioned to do it and it has its uses. However, it is not always called for. It doesn't support meditation practice very well, and in fact may create some irritation or unease. We can see in the comments from the students in this last class's sharing that they have in fact developed some Wise Mindfulness. They are less judgmental and have cultivated a greater capacity to be with whatever arises. How about you?

Wise Mindfulness also means we are practicing establishing mindfulness in the four fields referred to in the Buddha's comprehensive teaching on mindfulness, which we've explored in previous chapters. To recap, the four fields are:

- The body

- Feeling tones or categories of experience

- Mind-heart states

- The teachings of life, the Dharmas

As has been noted, throughout the *Discourse on the Four Foundations of Mindfulness* is the refrain that encourages paying attention, internally and externally, and to seeing the arising and passing away of all things. Without specifically knowing that Discourse, the people in the MBSR class are sharing their awareness of these fields, seeing into the impermanent nature of things, and, most importantly, acknowledging that when they have this awareness they suffer less.

Tenshin Roshi offers this great example of Wise Mindfulness in a very practical, everyday way. A working, active monastery, just like your home or place of work, has endless things that need to be done and the monks and residents have a lot to do to keep the place functioning. They aren't just sitting and bowing and chanting and lighting incense. They are chopping wood, cleaning bathrooms, responding to emails—just like us! So when people come to visit, Roshi kindly points out, "Mindfulness doesn't necessarily mean slowness. So when you are washing your dishes, look up and see how long the line behind you is. There are people in that line who have to be somewhere. Please extend your mindfulness to them!"

Mindfulness in this circumstance means that you can still be thorough, feel the water, and be fully present, and also be awake to the fact that the community needs you to move along. This expresses beautifully and simply the practice of internal mindfulness (what is happening inside of you) and external mindfulness (what is going on around you). It also brings home the point that mindfulness is not conceptual. It's not some idea or concept about what mindfulness looks like, someone in a dreamy, thoughtful state slowly washing her dishes. Rather, it's an intimate encounter with what is right in front of you, inside you, and around you in this very moment. That's not always so easy to do—our minds love to conceptualize, judge, concretize. These deep habits of mind are what we are seeing more clearly, and perhaps undoing, as we stick with our practice day in and day out, no matter what it looks like or feels like.

You're Only Telling Me About Concentration Now?

Yep, let's talk about concentration now. The eighth factor of the Eightfold Path is Wise Concentration. Concentration is also translated as "absorption," which I rather like.

From the beginning of an MBSR class, we are inviting concentration to develop when we focus on and experience the raisin as fully as possible. For some folks, it may be more possible than for others, whose minds may be quite naturally flooded with other preoccupations or wonderings about what the heck the raisin has to do with anything. Still, we're inviting some focused attention and asking folks to sustain it for a few chews.

Then, with the body scan we're inviting the attention to stay with various parts of the body, and seeing, sometimes quite shockingly, how much it wanders. No matter what the mind gets up to, we continue to invite it to stay. Over time, the less we judge and criticize it, the more it begins to calm down. Have you noticed this in yourself? We've certainly seen it in the MBSR class.

In terms of the Eightfold Path, concentration deepens our moment-to-moment experience. We place the attention and then ask it to remain for a while. This kind of sustained attention leads to some stability, which lends itself to clarity. Jon Kabat-Zinn uses the analogy that trying to see clearly without the stability that sustained practice offers is like trying to see through a telescope while we're situated on a water bed—we're not likely to see anything clearly, if at all.

When we're able to sustain attention, we are also able to see and feel the after-effects of our actions and our attitudes, and are then able to repair when needed. Conversely, if we do something unskillful and then rush off to the next thing, we might miss important feedback that leads to ethical and kind behavior.

On a very physical level, I've noticed a few times on retreat that when I have overeaten and there is a sitting period after lunch, I really get to feel how uncomfortable I am. This makes it a lot less likely to happen again, because I truly experience the consequences of my action. Because my attention is sustained, I am available to this feedback loop, and I remember it. Likewise, when I engage in even a small act of kindness and I stay present, I get feedback about how fulfilling it feels to be kind, which encourages me to continue to act in this way—not because I'm trying to be a certain kind of person, but because it feels good.

Concentration—that is, aiming and sustaining our attention with an attitude of kindness and curiosity—can loosen the grip of suffering, as we have seen with our class participants. An example of this is Brian, who joined us in class 2 with the dilemma of his failed hip replacement. This not only caused him great physical pain, it also plunged him into deep despair and fear, as he felt the loss of control and the loss of his formerly strong, "I'll take care of everyone" self. The very first time he tried the body scan and concentrated on the parts of his body, which included many parts that were not in pain, he was able to let go of his painful story and experience peace. This ability to focus his attention in this way grew and strengthened through the eight weeks, offering him a freedom he had not been able to find previously. In class 4 (see chapter 4) we practiced sitting meditation with awareness of breath—the very first concentration practice the Buddha taught. Carol reported that when she tried it, the knee pain that had been "bothering her all day" was still present, but her reaction to it had changed. She was not so distressed by it anymore—in other words, she found peace in the midst of discomfort, allowing it to be there while concentrating on her breath in the present moment and connecting with her wholeness. She was reunited with her whole self, not just isolated in her knee pain. That's one of the gifts of Wise Concentration.

However, concentration or absorption is not just for difficulties. It actually happens quite naturally when we are doing
things we love, like making music, playing with our dog, or
listening to our child tell a story. It may enhance our ability to
enjoy and appreciate the positive things in our lives, but not
necessarily. We can just as easily *not* be present while doing
things we enjoy, or would potentially enjoy if our minds weren't
so scattered and preoccupied. I've spent many a forest walk lost
in thought about work—until I remember to be where I am and
work later. So concentration can help us be more fully absorbed
in and alive to the joys of our lives. When I asked Tenshin
Roshi about absorption, he said, "I can be fully absorbed when
I'm working, parenting, practicing, and also when I am just
chilling. Instead of trying to relax and feeling guilty about it,
my energy is not drained away by being divided, and I enjoy
myself more." The feeling of not being "divided" is why absorption is often referred to as a way of being unified.

As for my question about *Wise* Concentration: I've been
thinking about a Dharma talk I heard once by Tempel Smith,
an amazing Dharma teacher, while on a retreat. He pointed
out that we can intensely concentrate and feel very clear when
we are filled with hatred, self-righteousness, or resentment.
Isn't that the truth? At least, as soon as he said it I recognized
it as true for me. We can hardly take our attention off something that is bugging us. Our attention can be like a laser beam
when it is filled with irritation, anger, even physical pain. That's
obviously not the kind of concentration we're going for!

That's why it's important that we have fostered the development of the other factors on the Eightfold Path, so we can
have Wise Concentration. We need our wise and kind intention, as well as our ethics, to know where and with what attitude to concentrate. Mindfulness helps us discern how we feel
if we are concentrating on something negative. When we're
absorbed with anger or worry, it feels very differently in the

body than if we are absorbed in the present moment without judgment or reactivity.

Absorption is said to lead to calm and peace, so if it is not doing this—and you would know this through the First and Third Foundations of Mindfulness—Mindfulness of the Body and Mindfulness of Mind-Heart States—you might want to regroup. See if you can use your practice to hold this difficulty differently, adding some space, inquiring into what is occurring with curiosity, and perhaps focusing on the breath for a while until enough calm develops so that you can see more clearly what is going on.

The Buddha also taught that concentration can be one-pointed (for instance, focusing on the left big toe) or wide and encompassing (for example, taking in the entire body). Developing one-pointed concentration can be very calming and stabilizing. In addition, it helps us in life—for example, when we have to give our full attention to one aspect of our work rather than to the whole project or the whole organization, or when we really need to zero in on solving a particular aspect of a larger issue. However, we may then need to zoom back out and see this one problem in its larger context. We can be concentrated and still have some flexibility of mind, which is actually very useful and applicable for how we function in daily life. We practice this in MBSR in various ways, as I showed above regarding the body scan—one part, the whole, moving back and forth. In the sitting meditation we focus on the breath and then on the whole body, on sounds and then thoughts, and then open out to the whole wide field of awareness itself in the "choiceless awareness" practice. Whether concentration is wide or narrow, we're still absorbed in what we *choose* to be absorbed in, rather than making our grocery list or preparing a speech.

Lastly, it is good to have a sense of why we are concentrating, framing it always in the overarching intention to be free from suffering. Thich Nhat Hanh suggests that we not use concentration to "run away from ourselves or our suffering." In other words, concentration is not meant to be a suppression technique or a distancing practice. Rather, when combined with mindfulness and kindness, it offers stability to actually face what we may need to face in order to be free.

What's Happening Now?

Let's see how these learnings are unfolding at this last class. After our discussion about the body scan, I lead a guided reflection on the whole program. "Taking a posture that embodies a sense of dignity and wakefulness, and feeling your own breathing. Now allowing yourself to reflect on why you came to the program, and what it has been like for you. What changes, if any, have you noticed? What could you give yourself credit for? Honoring your efforts and the way you have supported others just by being here. What is your experience right now?"

I invite them into pairs to share with each other some of what they have seen and learned. And you, dear reader, might also reflect on this. Has anything changed for you while reading this book and doing the practices?

I gaze around the circle, feeling my heart full of affection and great respect for these travelers. I overhear fragments: "I don't know what we will do without each other!" and "I'm going to ask Beth what she thinks." I wonder, about what? Sometimes during the last few classes people try and see if they can squeeze some definitive answers out of me, even "What is the meaning of life?" But I haven't given them any so far. Rather, I always point them back to their own experience, or invite them to "not know" for a while more together. I can't really say anything they don't already know or won't come to know. After all, while it is the end of the program, it is just the beginning of a lifetime of practice. I have great respect for and trust in their process. I don't want to add anything.

The Most Important Class

We settle into our large circle and I invite the students to share something about their experience with the entire group, if they wish. I realize that just as in class 1, Zach is sitting next to me. Instead of going last as he did eight weeks ago, he indicates that he wants to start us off.

"I came here at rock bottom, and I didn't want to be here. But something happened to me the first night. I listened to all of you—which in itself was a miracle." He smiles at his mom. "I'm not always so good at listening, but I really heard your stories and I realized that shit happens to everyone. And then I knew I wasn't alone, and even though I had no idea how mindfulness or meditation might help, I had the feeling that being with *you* would help. And it has. A lot. I'm talking with Brian about things maybe I could do, you know, to help others. Now that I think about it, I've learned some really useful things, like I can decide where to place my attention and when. I never knew I had that choice. I notice I can stick with things more. I was so upset at the beginning, I couldn't even read a page when we started, but I can concentrate better and I finished a whole book. And when the hard feelings come, the memories, I am nicer to myself. But when I think about what I got the most out of the class, it was the first class for sure, the first class is the most important class."

Eileen goes next. "You know, what surprised me the most was the fact that even though I'm not very good at meditation, I mean there's so much mind wandering—and to be honest, I still have trouble making time for it—I would definitely say the class has changed my life. I am much more present with the kids, which means I am more connected and having more fun. And even stuff I hate, like grading tests, which used to take me through a bag of Oreos and a lot of fuming about the horrible education system—I just do it now. One at a time, I focus on that one thing without all the extra thoughts and it flies by, no cookies required. Thank you all so much, you've all touched me deeply."

Zach and Eileen are clearly describing Wise Mindfulness and Wise Concentration. Because they've stuck with the practice, it has happened all on its own, unfolding organically. I can imagine that this might be happening for you as well, dear reader.

Joe stands up, with a stack of something in his hands. He turns and looks right at me. "Beth, I know I was kind of hard on you at times, I'm hard on everyone. You knew I had back pain and I was a grumpy old man, but what you might not know is I am an artist. I've been one all my life. After the all-day retreat I went home and started painting again for the first time in a long time. Here is what I created for all of you."

He then hands out shiny postcards covered with brilliant splashes of primary colors, brush strokes that appear to be dancing and flowing. One for each of us.

"Thank you, Joe," I say. "What is the painting called?"

"*Here.*"

"Well, guys, I'm at the end of my life. Not too much time to go, they tell me," says a pale, thin Alan. The calm radiating out from him is palpable. "This class gave me, gave us"—he looks at Norma and takes her hand—"the opportunity to really ask what we wanted to do with the time I had left, and we did it, we're doing it. That is a priceless gift. I feel so fortunate to have come at this particular time, so lucky to know all of you. We thank you all for your support and kindness and we wish the best for you."

Norma simply adds, "We love you all."

Renée says, "We love you, too." She looks around the room and pauses for a moment. "At the first class I said, 'Everyone has something.' Tonight I'll add, 'We're all in this together.' "

Ah, wisdom indeed.

It has happened again and yet it still feels completely fresh and new—this circle of Buddhas teaching me the Dharma. I truly am the lucky one.

And so, dear reader, please know we really are all in this together. You are not alone, and you too are a Buddha, you too are awake and whole and loved.

Chapter 10

THE DHARMA OF FOUR GOOD GARDENS: Cultivating Attitudes

Recently a local health care provider asked me about the classes I teach at the hospital. He didn't know anything about MBSR, mindfulness, Jon Kabat-Zinn, or the teachings of the Buddha. I told him briefly that these classes offer a way to educate people about stress and offer some options, including the development of skills that enhance our ability to cope more effectively with it.

"Stress, eh?" he said. "I imagine that must draw a particularly challenging population. How do *you* personally deal with their stress and your *own* stress?"

I deeply appreciated his question, it felt authentic and meaningful. This chapter is, in part, my answer to that question. As I've mentioned throughout this book, I sit in exam rooms, hospital rooms, and classrooms with people who are deeply suffering, often at times when I may have my own "full catastrophe" going on. So this question is something I have considered and practiced with a great deal.

Perhaps I also appreciated his question because I spent years *not* having an effective way to meet suffering wisely and with resilience, and it was *very* painful, leading to burnout and even despair. His question made me reflective, as good questions do. How do I deal with it? I practice, and I take refuge. I use all the practices we've explored up to this point. And more and more I find it difficult to discern the difference between anyone else's suffering and my own. As Renée said at the end of class 8, "We're all in this together." This perspective gives me greater ease and peace. Additionally, I rely on the following practices that we have not discussed yet, so here they are.

The Four Immeasurables

In this chapter, I want to offer you another traditional teaching that I hope you will find helpful on your journey. I know it's been extremely useful to me as a teacher, clinician, and human being on this earth, providing a sturdy and comforting raft as challenges arise. This teaching, like all the other Buddhist teachings, is not taught explicitly or ever referred to in MBSR, but I invite you to see where these teachings may have unfolded implicitly, through embodiment and awareness.

This teaching consists of practices known as the Four Brahma Viharas, which is translated as Divine Abodes. They are also called the Four Immeasurables, which is the term I will use hereafter. They are:

1. *Metta*: Loving-Kindness or Boundless Friendliness, a way of cultivating our inherent good will;

2. *Karuna*: Compassion, the natural response of the heart when our Metta, our good will, specifically meets suffering;

3. *Mudita*: Sympathetic or Empathetic Joy, the capacity to take true joy in the happiness of others.

4. *Upekkha*: Equanimity—a way of riding the vicissitudes of life, with all of its sorrows and beauty, while maintaining some balance, clarity, and presence, by drawing on the practices and wisdom of the other three Immeasurables.

You may recall that with mindfulness practice, there are formal ways to practice (sitting meditation, body scan, walking meditation) and informal practices, the way we weave kind, curious awareness into everyday life—eating, working, parenting, and playing. The Four Immeasurables also have formal and informal ways of practicing. In this chapter I intend to mainly present the *feeling and intention* and everyday application of them, emphasizing the informal aspect. The formal versions, both written and audio, are accessible at www .newharbinger.com/39164. (For written guidance, click "Practicing the Immeasurables with Phrases." For audio guidance, click "Track 6: Metta," "Track 7: Karuna," "Track 8: Mudita," and "Track 9: Upekkha.")

The reason this chapter is called Four Good Gardens is because it is important to understand that this teaching is not about adding anything to ourselves that we don't already have. Rather, it's about watering, fertilizing, and bringing sunlight and oxygen to our innate capacities to care—capacities that sometimes get short shrift in our busy lives—so they can grow and blossom. So let's go gardening.

Learning the Four Immeasurables Through the Back Door

I was fortunate to learn about the Four Immeasurables in part from Sharon Salzberg, who has led the way in bringing these ancient teachings, which she learned in Burma, to the West.

In this section I am going to use a different population from the "general population" who come to my MBSR classes, because this particular class really stretched me out of my comfort zone, which I have found makes for deep learning. Years ago I was asked to teach an MBSR adaptation to a group at a homeless women's rehabilitation shelter. There were many challenges working at the shelter—starting with the facts that the class was mandatory and most of the women did not want to be there; that many of the women were very newly sober or clean from addiction or had varying degrees of mental health issues; and that they were deeply and understandably exhausted. The first time I faced the large group, I was not looking out on happy or expectant faces, to put it mildly. And even though I had prepared the adaptation with my mentors at the UMASS Center for Mindfulness and thought I knew something, I quickly realized I was in over my head.

After the first week with this group, I was able to attend a weekend retreat on the Four Immeasurables with Sharon Salzberg. I hung on to every word and practiced as we do when we're stretched! The confluence of this challenging class with the retreat proved to be such a valuable learning ground that I offer it to you in this context.

Metta: Loving-Kindness or Boundless Friendliness

Buddhist scholar John Peacock says that "boundless friendliness" is a more accurate translation of the Pali word *Metta*, so often translated as "loving-kindness." I personally resonate with his translation, but see what fits for you. Many of us have strong associations with the word "love," perhaps connecting it to romantic love, or to our strong attachments to our families or to just a few people we're close to. Or even "I love chocolate." Metta is not that. Hint: the word "boundless" is a clue to what it *is*. And "friendliness" may feel more open and less charged than "love."

We have minds that work well with opposites, so the Buddha taught that each Immeasurable has what are called near and far enemies ("enemy" simply meaning something that gets in the way). The far enemy of Metta is pretty easy to spot: hatred or ill will. You'll probably know when you are cultivating that because of how it makes you feel. As one current saying goes, "Cultivating resentment is like taking rat poison and waiting for the rat to die." Yep, that's what ill will feels like.

The near enemy of Metta is a little sneakier to catch because it may feel good—in part. This near enemy is a more attached and conditional kind of love, as in "I'll love you if you do these things in a certain way and make me feel secure." It includes a sense of ownership. Think of a Valentine card with "Be mine" boldly on the cover, or love songs wailing "You're mine" or "If you leave me, I'll die." (But no pressure.) These thoughts or feelings are called an enemy of Metta because when we're in the midst of them, it's difficult to actually offer the kind of unconditional friendliness that has the potential to shine on everyone and everything, which Metta cultivates. I know how the near enemy works because I've experienced it.

When I heard about the near enemy of Metta that weekend during the retreat with Sharon Salzberg, I felt a little "ping" of recognition inside me. As I said, I was struggling with the class at the women's shelter and felt I was not doing very well. I was feeling frustrated, inadequate, and a bit lost.

As Sharon spoke, I saw where I was getting caught. I was unconsciously attached to an outcome. I wanted the women to have a particular experience, the relief of suffering, and my friendliness toward them was partly conditional on them having that experience.

It was so helpful to see that! When I got home from the retreat, I changed course. I started to get to the shelter early, so as to have dinner with the women and learn more about them. I brought art supplies and music, completely letting go of the curriculum. I simply befriended them without expecting anything in return. Whew! That was somewhat better. This part of the gardening process, seeing what is in the way, is kind of like rototilling or plowing, taking weeds and old plants and turning them into the soil, where they become fertilizer for the crop we want to grow. If we learn from what awareness and good teachers allow us to see, nothing is lost, it's simply composted.

Cultivating the Metta Garden

In the practice of Metta, there is an invitation to evoke a feeling of friendliness, perhaps while quietly sitting or lying down, bringing to mind the image or felt sense of someone or something you dearly love, a relatively uncomplicated relationship—animals definitely included! Someone who, when you think of him or her, might easily evoke a smile. As you see or feel the presence of this being, see if the feeling of love, appreciation, and care is felt in the body. Is there warmth? Tingling? In the belly or chest? However you experience it, allow it to grow and radiate throughout your body, seeing if it can fill your entire being and then even go beyond it. Spend some time in silence and stillness, radiating this good will toward yourself and out to other beings. You may offer it to people you know, to people you don't know, and to all living creatures and to the earth itself, trying it as an experiment in "boundlessness."

In some versions of the practice, we nourish the feelings of good will with simple phrases that are repeated silently to oneself. They may include gentle wishes for safety, happiness, health, well-being, and ease—in other words, freedom from suffering. For example, "May I and all beings live with ease and well-being." Both audio and written downloads can be found at www.newharbinger.com/39164. (For written guidance, click "Practicing the Immeasurables with Phrases." For audio guidance, click "Track 6: Metta.")

Please know that there is no one way to feel if or when you practice Metta. You may feel good, or nothing at all, or even the opposite: sadness or anger may arise. There is a saying I learned from my colleagues Christopher Germer and Kristin Neff, who developed the Mindful Self-Compassion program: "Love reveals anything unlike itself." Meaning that sometimes when the suggestion to feel or connect with loving-kindness is offered, we may quickly go to times and places where we did *not* feel loved. This is a natural response, and nothing is wrong if this occurs.

If you find yourself feeling angry or sad while practicing Metta, be kind and return to the breath, or just let the practice go. Alternatively, like me with my near-enemy "ping" moment, you can learn a lot about yourself by trying to stick with it, without forcing but *with* curiosity. Simply and kindly bring friendliness to the lack of friendliness and see if you can befriend that. You know what is right for you. If you need help, talk to a wise friend or teacher.

Notes on Loving-Kindness to Self

The classic Buddhist instructions ask you to begin with yourself, which, in the time and place when this was originally practiced, made sense and was considered the easiest place to start. In fact the Buddha outright said: "You can search the entire universe and you will never find anyone more deserving of your love than you are yourself." However, in this time, many people find it difficult to start with themselves. I mention this so that you will not feel alone if this is the case for you. If you do encounter this problem as you try the practices, you might investigate it with kindness, perhaps working with a teacher, friend, or therapist. Many of us were not taught that it's crucial and actually necessary to offer kindness to ourselves. If this is a big obstacle for you (and it certainly was for me), I highly recommend the teachings of Christopher Germer and Kristin Neff on Mindful Self-Compassion, listed in the "Recommended Readings" at the end of this book. These teachings, along with the Four Immeasurables, have been immensely helpful to me.

One last instruction about the practice of Metta that is very important, and that may also be applied to the other three Immeasurables, is that this is not a practice intended to cover pain or to move us away from our challenges. In fact, the

Buddha's original teachings on Metta came as instructions to his monks as a way to work with their fears and aversions. He asked them to turn toward that which frightened them, to face it bravely and offer good will. This practice is still alive today because it proved to be so effective. In this spirit, it may help to include the phrase, "May I be peaceful *in the midst of whatever is happening*." This is a way of acknowledging that while life does include difficulties, there is a gentle possibility of peace right in their midst.

The Everyday Practice of Metta

As with mindfulness practice, it's important to set aside time to practice Metta when there is not much else going on. But just as we also practice bringing mindfulness into eating, walking, parenting, and so on, we can also practice Metta on the fly, right in the midst of things. For example, when I am getting impatient in the TSA line at the airport, I offer Metta to myself and everyone around me. I also do it on the airplane and the bus. It has really changed my travel experience. Try it in the grocery store, or to strangers walking down the street.

Karuna: Watering the Seeds of Compassion

The literal translation of *Karuna* is a "quivering of the heart" that arises in response to suffering. If Metta embodies the wish for all beings to be happy under all conditions, then Karuna is what happens when this good will encounters suffering—the heart wishes for the alleviation of suffering, without commanding or demanding that it be so. It is a gentle inclination of heart and mind.

The far enemy of compassion is cruelty or the wish for harm. The near enemy of compassion is a sense of being overwhelmed, of feeling the suffering with the other person so intensely that one is in too much pain to be of much use. It is also pity or sympathy, bringing with it a sense of separation, as in "I feel so sorry for you over there."

At that first weekend exploration of the Four Immeasurables, as soon as I heard about the near enemy of compassion I felt that little "ping" of recognition again. I saw immediately that the intensity of the suffering in the women's shelter was over-whelming me, just as the suffering of my patients or my loved ones sometimes did. Without the buoyancy that Metta gives us, it's possible to drown in another's suffering. At least I have felt that way many times. Have you? Feeling the suffering without the unconditional wish for relief (not a demand, mind you) is indeed overwhelming.

That's why, as with the practice of Metta, we start the prac-tice of Karuna by offering compassion to ourselves. It *is* difficult to bear witness to the suffering of others. We can invite com-passion for ourselves simply because this is so, and because we have our own suffering, even if it might pale in comparison to that of others. We start with ourselves because we're human beings. When we remember this, we are more available to be present for the suffering of others. Jack Kornfield says, "If your compassion does not include yourself, it is incomplete." Karuna invites us to have less separation between our suffering and that of others, while giving us something strong to hold on to.

After this powerful learning and before I went back to the shelter, I reflected on a quotation I have above my desk, attrib-uted to an aboriginal activist group: "If you have come here to help me, you are wasting your time. But if you have come because your liberation is bound up with mine, then let us work together." I remembered that I wasn't there to "help" those women in the shelter, but because my suffering and my freedom *are* bound up with theirs. So I practiced offering compassion to myself, starting with compassion for the fact that I had been overwhelmed, and when I began to feel a bit stronger I offered compassion to those women, and then to all beings suffering from the effects of poverty and violence in ever widening circles. As a result of this practice, I began to feel more stable and present with them and myself, and we began to have some real connection together.

The Practice of Karuna with Phrases

Like Metta, this practice has phrases you can work with. Both audio and written downloads can be found at www.newharbinger.com/39164. (For written guidance, click "Practicing the Immeasurables with Phrases." For audio guidance, click "Track 7: Karuna.")

Checking in with Compassion

One way you can check in with yourself about the practice is to see if you feel like you are running out of compassion. If you do, this might be a time to see if you are including yourself, or if you might have slipped into the near enemy territory. Perhaps you have heard the expression "compassion fatigue"? I once heard a leader in the Stanford "Compassion Cultivation Training" program say that she did not feel that there actually was compassion fatigue, only outcome fatigue. This really captured my attention; I felt a deep recognition of truth. Can we feel compassion without expecting anything specific to occur?

Here's where being grounded in mindfulness is really helpful. Let me share how it works for me. I feel the fatigue or the sense of being overwhelmed arise in awareness. I might feel it in my body first, as heaviness or sinking. Then I can kindly check in with myself and offer myself compassion, because I have gotten a little lost. I might ask what my expectations are (they can be very sneaky sometimes), and after I see those expectations I simply begin anew. I don't have to blame myself or feel like a failure, although this was my old go-to position.

This practice has elasticity and is endlessly forgiving. Whatever we see in ourselves and others can be included in the embrace of compassion. Compassion truly is our natural response to suffering, *and* it can be useful to intentionally practice it, especially toward ourselves.

Everyday Practice of Karuna

In your day-to-day life, when you find yourself suffering or are in the presence of suffering in another, you might try breathing in the feeling of compassion for yourself by imagining carrying in a kind word or a sense of warmth on the inhale, and then breathing out compassion for another on the exhale. This practice is part of the Mindful Self-Compassion program. You might try it when you're stuck in traffic—simply feeling compassion because we're all in this traffic jam together.

Mudita: Shining Sunlight on Joy

Mudita is "the wholesome attitude of rejoicing in the happiness of all beings." It is the response of the heart when our Metta, our good will, encounters joy. Have you ever found yourself laughing simply because you heard someone else laughing, even a total stranger? Or smiling when you see a smile? This is spontaneous Mudita! It feels good, right? It's a way to find joy any time and anywhere. However, the idea that this could be actively invited and cultivated may be new to you. At least it was to me, even though I was very familiar with the feeling of Mudita when it was present.

As with the other Immeasurables, Mudita rests on this idea that we are not so separate and that our suffering and our joy are "bound up" with each other. His Holiness the Dalai Lama says Mudita is actually "enlightened self-interest." If we can take joy in the joy of another and there are seven billion people on the planet, then this increases our opportunities for happiness by—well, let's do the math: seven billion. That's a lot more happiness.

In our current culture and our time, we may tend to think of *my* happiness and *your* happiness, and perhaps even think there might not be quite enough to go around. There is a feeling I sometimes experience after I go on Facebook, seeing friends and people I don't even know on their fabulous vacations with loads of smiling children around them, having just returned from their triathlon and cooked a colorful, healthy meal. Whatever that feeling is, it's not Mudita. Have you ever felt that way? It does not feel good. This feeling may be the far enemy of Mudita, which is jealousy or envy. But sometimes this feeling is one of the near enemies of Mudita, which is comparing your life to others, and stems from the belief that there is a limited supply of happiness.

Another near enemy of Mudita is exuberance. So how does that work? Perhaps we have a strong need for someone else to be happy so that we can be happy. If we're a little low on compassion, we may have such a strong wish for their happiness that when they have some, there's a sense of "Oh, thank God, you're happy, I can relax now." Or perhaps we get overexcited about someone's accomplishment, which may actually feel like pressure to them. Like the other near enemies, it may involve some degree of expectation. This is good to know and to bring into awareness.

When I learned that a near enemy of Mudita was exuberance, I felt that "ping" thing again, and took a look with compassionate awareness at where I had been caught by exuberance working at the shelter. When I first heard about the grant to do this work, I definitely felt happy. I knew it would have many new challenges. I reached out to my colleagues and friends at the UMASS Center for Mindfulness who had worked with similar populations for guidance about adaptations. Still, I was excited, and naïve.

First, it's very different teaching a mandatory class than one people have signed up for. But there were many other challenges that I was blind to because of my exuberance. Exuberance even presented an obstacle with the women who *were* getting something out of the class, who appreciated it, because, I realized later, I was overly attached to that.

Once I began to spend more time with the women outside of class, I learned a lot more about their lives. One got a job interview, another one was hired, one was getting her GED. One had a good visit with her daughter. I began to take joy in their happiness and successes in realms that had nothing to do with the class or my presence there. This gave me great sustenance and encouragement to go in and face the group, while letting go of expectations for anything in particular to happen. And as weeks passed, when people said things like "I'm using mindful walking to the bus stop, it's really helped me not stress so much about being late!" or "I'm making fewer mistakes at work" or "I noticed the urge to go use [drugs], and I didn't," I could gently wish for their happiness to continue without clinging to any expectation. And letting go of overexuberance helped me to be with the feelings of sadness that arose the next week, when it was *not* like that—when, for example, that same participant who had shared her success did go and use drugs and was no longer able to stay at the shelter.

The Practice of Mudita with Phrases

Both audio and written downloads can be found at www .newharbinger.com/39164. (For written guidance, click "Practicing the Immeasurable with Phrases." For audio guidance, click "Track 8: Mudita.")

Everyday Mudita

Sometimes when I am out picking up a coffee before a class and am perhaps feeling kind of flat or low, I might spot some folks who are clearly having a good time. As I hear their laughter I pause and let this sink in, while wishing for their happiness to continue and grow. It actually gives me more energy than the cup of coffee. Try noticing joy around you. It may simply be a dog wagging its tail or a child gleefully running. When you notice it, pause and wish them happiness. See what happens. It's also a great antidote to the "Facebook feeling."

Upekkha: Nourishing the Soil of Equanimity

Upekkha is translated as "equanimity," which is defined as "composure and evenness of temper under stress." It begins with understanding that what the Buddha called the worldly winds—praise and blame, success and failure, gain and loss, pleasure and pain—can change quickly, and we don't have to be blown away by them. In discussing this Immeasurable, Insight Meditation teacher Gil Fronsdal offers a more collo-quial sense of Upekkha used in India: "to see with patience." I love that! Upekkha includes seeing the long view. I once heard it referred to as a "long loving look at the real."

The near enemy of Upekkha is indifference. We may feel that distancing ourselves and observing from a distance creates equanimity. Conversely, there may also be some fear that we'll lose our passion for things and people we love if we're too equa-nimous. I've heard some people express a fear that life may become flat or cool with equanimity. Equanimity is actually warm and its stability allows us to move closer to life, to love and live deeply, because we're resting on a foundation of the capacity to restore balance when we lose it. There have been times in my physician assistant career when I've been burned out enough to unknowingly retreat to indifference, feeling that it would somehow protect me. It didn't. When it came to my work at the shelter, learning about indifference did not create that "ping." I cared deeply about the women and my efforts there.

I did, however, feel a loud "ping" when it came to the far enemy of equanimity, which is being off balance. As I faced the challenge of the work at the shelter, I had been thrown off center, my nervous system was really activated, and I was having trouble finding my way back. In a question-and-answer period during the retreat I uncharacteristically grabbed the microphone to ask for help. I briefly described the situation, and the first thing Sharon said to me was, "Expand your time line. You don't know what seeds are being planted or when they will bloom."

I took those words back with me to the women's shelter and realized that I was planting new ways of seeing and skills for emotional regulation that might kick in for someone at a critical moment long after the class finished. I realized that this was certainly true in my own life. Things I wasn't ready to hear at the time showed up and sustained me years later. Those words, "Expand your timeline," have stayed with me for many years and have become my "equanimity mantra" when I feel off center. The traditional teachings point us to the fact that all beings' lives are made up of many choices and actions, and we can't possibly know the whole picture. Our wishes for them may only impact them a little, if at all, and the impact depends more on their own conditioning, actions, and choices. We can't control anyone's life. But we can be disappointed, frustrated, hurt—and still keep our hearts open with equanimity.

Practicing Equanimity with Phrases

Please go to www.newharbinger.com/39164 for audio and written guidance. (For written guidance, click "Practicing the Immeasurables with Phrases." For audio guidance, click "Track 9: Equanimity.")

The Everyday Practice of Equanimity

The Buddha taught that one way to support equanimity is to surround yourself with wise, equanimous people. Nowadays this might include being protective of what media input you take in. Notice how certain interactions feel—how they encourage making wise choices that nourish a feeling of stability—and notice how certain other interactions don't. During your day when you feel activated and off center, particularly around someone else's life and struggles, notice how you're feeling with mindful awareness, focus on the breath, and then remember that you don't know the whole story. Then expand your timeline!

The Garden of Embodiment

One of the most powerful ways I have learned about these qualities of Metta, Karuna, Mudita, and Upekkha has been through watching them naturally unfold in the MBSR classrooms, even without being explicitly mentioned. I see that they truly are our natural state. When with our practice we get a few things out of the way, they emerge. In the class we've followed in this book we've seen our participants offer good will to themselves and each other, have compassion when someone is struggling, and celebrate each other's joys. We've seen them find balance in the midst of whatever is happening.

I have learned equally powerful lessons in the Immeasurables from my teachers and my partner Hugh. When I am in their presence during times when I am deeply upset, what I feel is their wordless wish for my well-being. I experience their kindness and compassion. And, I suspect, sometimes a degree of sympathetic joy because they know that I am touching my experience deeply and that is part of the path to freedom.

Finally, I have felt truly held by their equanimity, in that no matter how much I feel I am falling apart, I don't see any alarm or worry on their faces. I feel that they trust my wholeness and my strength as they do with anyone, not just me. This, most of all, has allowed me to remember my wholeness for myself, even at some of the lowest moments. This is the embodied Immeasurable.

Trusting the Earth

Remember Linda from the introduction? Her life had been turned completely upside down by illness, but through her MBSR class and Dharma study and practice, she had found equanimity, in spite of not finding a cure for the illness itself. I saw her recently at a Dharma talk I gave at our Insight Center in Palm Springs, still rolling along with her service dog Kiki in front. She let go of the walker and threw her arms around me, smiling. "I have something for you," she said, and handed me a tiny box. Inside was a silver pendant with the word HOPE written on it.

"Thank you, it's beautiful," I said.

"That's what you gave me," she said.

"Well, I think you had a whole lot to do with that," I replied. "No one can practice for you, right?"

"Right," she agreed. "Did you hear about the group I started for chronic pain patients? We meet here on Tuesdays."

"Yes, I did. What an important offering, Linda."

"I just want to pass the hope and the peace on, you know?"

You never know what seeds are being planted—you really never know. But I think we can trust the earth to bloom when it blooms.

One of the aspects of living in the mountains here is that we have been touched by forest fires many times. One fall there was a particularly bad fire that left our home standing but the land black and scorched. Unbeknownst to me, Hugh planted hundreds of daffodil, crocus, and tulip bulbs. He quietly cared for them and then nature did the rest, covering them in snow during the winter and shining sun on them on other days. To my surprise, in April our property was ablaze with yellow, red, and purple amidst the black and gray. I hadn't known what was underground, and the colorful sight filled me with delight.

Our practice is like that. May your practice nourish and sustain you during dark and light times, may you be surprised by what is going on underground. May you trust in your wholeness, and may you appreciate the flowers of your own good heart.

ACKNOWLEDGMENTS

One of the strongest themes of this book is the vital need for community and connection with wise friends in order to live a meaningful life and stay true to our values. The process of writing this book mirrors that need completely. I have not done it alone; just as my practice has been guided and nurtured by many souls, so too has the writing of this book.

There would not be a book with my name on it, and the words "Dharma" or "Buddha" in the title and the text, without my many years of working with a truly great Zen teacher: Charles Tenshin Fletcher Roshi, Abbot of Yokoji Zen Mountain Center. While I have had the opportunity to sit many retreats with him, hear his weekly Dharma talks, train residentially with him, and meet one-on-one with him, just as importantly, the way he lives is his ultimate teaching. An active working monastery requires a lot of "off the cushion" practice. I learn from Tenshin Roshi in the way he cares for his family, the community, the land—and me. He holds the space for thousands of people to find refuge at Yokoji, whether by formal teaching or by driving a tractor to make sure the road is clear so we can get to the Zen center. Gratitude to him, and to all who live and practice at Yokoji, especially Susan Tipton and David Blackwell.

When it came to the Foreword, there was only one name on my list: my MBSR mentor and Zen teacher, Melissa Blacker. She balances clarity and kindness in a way unlike anyone else I have ever met. She has shown me that there are really many streams to one river, and she lives, breathes, and embodies that big river. Thank you, Melissa, for "seeing me."

Deep gratitude to Jon Kabat-Zinn for his vision and commitment to bringing this transformative work to the world, including to the very place where I worked in medicine and to me personally. He is the embodiment of everything I have tried to express in this book. I thank him for reading drafts of the manuscript and supporting and encouraging this project.

Chris Germer not only taught me the practice of self-compassion, he helped me get through the sometimes painful editorial process by reading early drafts with care and sharing his extensive experience in writing and publishing. He and Kristin Neff have made a huge impact on my life, both by fostering my personal practice and my development as a Mindful Self-Compassion teacher, and through their selfless commitment to reducing suffering in this world. This thanks extends to all of my MSC family.

David Rynick has been my coach and Zen teacher for many years, through some very challenging and wondrous times, and has lovingly (sometimes with a sword of clarity) walked every step of this path with me. He is everything you could ever want in a guide. Deep bows to you, dear friend.

Oceanic gratitude to Larry Yang, my friend, teacher, and always-present sounding board. He is the living spirit of inclusiveness and inspires me every day to live with more integrity.

My understanding of the Dharma (of life) has been influenced greatly by my retreat teachers, Thich Nhat Hanh, Jack Kornfield, Sharon Salzberg, Sylvia Boorstein, Christina Feldman, John Peacock, Pema Chodron, Cheri Huber, and Trudy Goodman. I am blessed by you all. I also thank Joseph Goldstein for his clear and thorough teachings on the Four Foundations of Mindfulness through books and talks.

I have been guided and held by my beloved teachers and colleagues at the UMASS Center for Mindfulness: Saki Santorelli, Florence Meleo-Meyer, Lynn Koerbel, and Bob Stahl. You are living examples of truth and beauty.

As important as everyone above, the person equally responsible for my development into an MBSR teacher is Susan Heggie. As the former director of the Center for Healthy Living at Eisenhower Medical Center, Susan got MBSR into the hospital and then supported the program in every way possible. It was through her work that hundreds of people were able to access MBSR and I got to teach it! She also taught me to be a better public speaker and held me to a high standard, as well as becoming a beloved friend. I am also deeply grateful to the many clinicians who referred patients to the program and, most importantly, took the class for themselves: Dr. Christopher Flores, Dr. Rita Stec, and Dr. Robert Edleberg.

To my tribe of early readers, supporters, and cherished friends, Adrienne Beattie, Anne Twohig, Beth Sternlieb, Denise Dempsey, Michelle Becker, Steve Hickman, Jon Aaron, and Christiane Wolf: I could not have done it without you. As I look at this list I feel like the luckiest woman in the world to count these people as my friends—they are all living examples of the Dharma with whom I also have the privilege of co-teaching.

Gratitude to my wonderful team of editors: Mary Jane Ryan, who brought not only her extensive editorial and publishing expertise to the work, but her personal practice and wisdom, always offered so kindly; and to the compassionate, skilled team at New Harbinger, who inspired the book and held it straight and true: Jess O'Brien, Clancy Drake, Vicraj Gill, and Ken Knabb.

Robin Hinaman, my dearest friend and sister, painstakingly and patiently went through the final draft with me for hours at a time, sometimes just quietly holding the phone while I figured something out in her loving presence. Her joy about and deep belief in the project carried me through many days of doubt. Ian Challis brought his true Dharma eye to the work and sat side by side with me to hammer things out, making it thoroughly enjoyable. Plus, he brought fresh bread and chocolate! Lynn Koerbel edited the chapters on ethics, as of course she would. That is who she is. She is a dear, true sister and mentor.

Thank you to all the fine institutions who have supported MBSR in the world (and supported me as a teacher): the UMASS Center for Mindfulness; the Integrative Center for Medicine at UC Irvine; and especially Laurie Macaulay, Dr. Don Maurer, and Dr. Cameron Neece, at Loma Linda, who opened the door to us in research.

Thank you to the current and former Board of Directors at Insight Community of the Desert, who entrusted me to be the Guiding Teacher and who honor and humble me with their dedication to the sangha and the world.

Special thanks to Allen Grodsky, who was right there for me when I needed him for a particular issue. And to Dr. Mark Branson, who brought his many years of writing and publishing experience to encourage me (at a great bakery), for his deep and wide wisdom in all areas human, and for his friendship.

Huge thanks to my forever friend Joey Taylor, who always said, "Honey, you can write and you must!" She made me numerous meals, welcomed me into her home for weeks on end (and always has), and was my first compassion teacher through her great heart and soul.

I am fortunate to have a wonderful big brother, Kevin Mulligan, who always has my back and who has brought his kind understanding to my struggles, and his belief in me to the overcoming of them.

Thank you to my friend Jazzmyn, who listened to early chapters, made me laugh at myself, and most of all loves me. Bearing witness to your honest process through ovarian cancer keeps me grounded in what really matters.

How to say thank you to my life, work, and play partner, Hugh O'Neill, who patiently lived with this troublesome demanding third party (this book) in our household for two years? While I was holed up with my computer, he made us both many cups of tea and brought his great gift of Irish humor and storytelling to the process of writing and to my life—all while he continued to teach MBSR to folks day after day, week after week. He inspires me, encourages me, and rubs my feet. He is also the smartest person I know, in all the ways that really matter.

And deepest thanks to all the participants who have crossed my path in MBSR classes, Dharma centers, and on retreats. You are all my teachers.

GLOSSARY

The following are terms the reader may or may not be familiar with. For clarity, here are the working definitions as intended by the author.

Three Characteristics of Existence:

1. Impermanence

2. Suffering

3. Non-Self

Three Refuges:

1. The Buddha

2. The Dharma

3. The Sangha

Four Foundations of Mindfulness:

1. Mindfulness of the Body

2. Mindfulness of Feeling Tones

3. Mindfulness of Mind (or of Mind-Heart States)

4. Mindfulness of Dharmas

Four Noble Truths:

1. We all suffer

2. There is a cause of suffering

3. There is an end to suffering

4. The Eightfold Path

Four Immeasurables:

1. Metta

2. Karuna

3. Mudita

4. Upekkha

Five Precepts:

1. Not harming living things

2. Not taking what is not given

3. Refraining from sexual misconduct

4. Refraining from lying or gossip

5. Not taking intoxicating substances

Five Hindrances:

1. Restlessness or worry

2. Sensual desire or craving

3. Anger or ill will

4. Sloth or torpor

5. Doubt

Eightfold Path:

1. Wise View: insight into the true nature of reality

2. Wise Intention: cultivating renunciation, good will, and harmlessness

3. Wise Speech: using speech compassionately

4. Wise Action: ethical conduct, manifesting compassion

5. Wise Livelihood: making a living through ethical and nonharmful means

6. Wise Effort: cultivating wholesome qualities, releasing unwholesome qualities

7. Wise Mindfulness: whole body-and-mind awareness

8. Wise Concentration: through meditation practice, seeing deeply into the nature of reality, with stability of mind-heart

Buddha: the awakened one

Citta: mind-heart

Dharma: the Buddha's teachings and the teachings of life

Dukkha: suffering, dissatisfaction

Karuna: compassion

Kinhin: walking meditation in the Zen tradition

Metta: boundless friendliness or loving-kindness

Mudita: sympathetic joy

Nibbana (or *Nirvana*): extinguishing

Samma: wise

Sati: mindfulness

Satipatthana Sutta: Discourse on the Four Foundations of Mindfulness

Tanha: craving, unquenchable thirst

Upekkha: equanimity

Vedana: feeling tones—pleasant, unpleasant, neutral

RECOMMENDED READINGS AND RESOURCES

Books

Anâlayo. 2003. *Satipatthana: The Direct Path to Realization.* Cambridge, UK: Windhorse.

Bodhi, B. 1994. *The Noble Eightfold Path: Way to the End of Suffering.* Onalaska, WA: Pariyati.

Fletcher, C., & Scott, D. 2001. *The Way of Zen.* New York: St. Martin's Press.

Germer, C. 2009. *The Mindful Path to Self-Compassion: Freeing Yourself from Destructive Thoughts and Emotions.* New York: Guilford.

Gethin, R. 1998. *The Foundations of Buddhism.* Oxford, UK: Oxford University Press.

Goldstein, J. 2013. *Mindfulness: A Practical Guide to Awakening.* Boulder, CO: Sounds True.

Kabat-Zinn, J. 2013. *Full Catastrophe Living.* New York: Bantam.

Kabat-Zinn, J. 2011. "Some Reflections on the Origins of MBSR, Skillful Means, and the Trouble with Maps." *Contemporary Buddhism* 12: 281–306.

Kabat-Zinn, J., & Williams, J. 2013. *Mindfulness: Diverse Perspectives on Its Meaning, Origins, and Applications.* Abingdon, Oxon: Routledge.

Kornfield, J. 2008. *The Wise Heart: A Guide to the Universal Teachings of Buddhist Psychology.* New York: Bantam.

Neff, K. 2011. *Self-Compassion: The Proven Power of Being Kind to Yourself.* New York: HarperCollins.

Nhat Hanh, Thich. 1998. *The Heart of the Buddha's Teaching: Transforming Suffering into Peace, Joy, and Liberation.* Berkeley, CA: Parallax.

Ryan, T. 2012. *A Mindful Nation.* Carlsbad, CA: Hay House.

Salzberg, S. 1995. *Loving-Kindness: The Revolutionary Art of Happiness.* Boston: Shambala.

Practice Resources

Reading is great, but you might also want to sit a retreat for "inside-out learning." These are just a few of the places you can practice in residential retreat. Or find a local sitting group to support your practice and hear Dharma talks. Look for an Insight Meditation center or Zen center near you.

Boundless Way Temple/Worcester Zen Center, Worcester, MA: http://www.worcesterzen.org/. Sit with Melissa Myozen Blacker Roshi and David Dae An Rynick Roshi.

Insight Meditation Society, Barre, MA: www.dharma.org.

Mindful Way: Mindfulness-Based Training Programs and Retreats (an affiliate of the UMASS Center for Mindfulness). Various locations in the United States and Europe: www.mindful-way.com. Sit with Beth Joshi Mulligan and Hugh O'Neill.

Spirit Rock Insight Meditation Center, Woodacre, CA: http://www.spiritrock.org/.

Yokoji Zen Mountain Center, Mountain Center, CA: www.zmc.org. Sit with Charles Tenshin Fletcher Roshi.

Online Dharma talks: www.dharmaseed.org.

Mindfulness Research Resources

American Mindfulness Research Association (AMRA), a comprehensive data base with monthly updates: www.goamra.org.

UMASS Center for Mindfulness: www.umassmed.edu/cfm. Click on the "Research" tab.

Beth Ann Mulligan, PA-C, graduated magna cum laude from the Duke University School of Medicine physician assistant program in 1982, and has practiced primary care medicine with diverse populations for the past thirty years. She is a certified mindfulness-based stress reduction (MBSR) teacher and international teacher trainer for the University of Massachusetts Medical School Center for Mindfulness, as well as a certified mindful self-compassion (MSC) teacher and international teacher trainer. She teaches MBSR, MSC, and mindful eating at the Susan Samueli Center for Integrative Medicine and at InsightLA, and has been a presenter at the International Scientific Conference on Mindfulness. The Guiding Dharma teacher at Insight Community of the Desert, and a longtime senior student at Yokoji Zen Mountain Center, she leads meditation retreats across the country.

In 1993, foreword writer **Melissa Blacker** joined the staff of the University of Massachusetts Medical School Center for Mindfulness, founded by Jon Kabat-Zinn. Until 2012, she was a member of the mindfulness-based stress reduction (MBSR) teaching staff, associate director of the Stress Reduction Clinic, and director of professional training programs. Blacker offers private instruction in mindfulness meditation, and is also available for group workshops, classes, and silent mindfulness meditation retreats.

MORE BOOKS *from*
NEW HARBINGER PUBLICATIONS

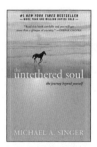

**YOGA & THE PURSUIT
OF HAPPINESS**

A Guide to Finding Joy
in Unexpected Places

ISBN 978-1626252875 / US $16.95

BUDDHA'S BRAIN

The Practical Neuroscience
of Happiness,
Love & Wisdom

ISBN 978-1572246959 / US $17.95

THE UNTETHERED SOUL

The Journey Beyond Yourself

ISBN 978-1572245372 / US $16.95

**FALLING IN LOVE WITH
WHERE YOU ARE**

A Year of Prose and Poetry
on Radically Opening Up to
the Pain & Joy of Life

ISBN 978-1908664396 / US $16.95

🌀 NON-DUALITY PRESS
An Imprint of New Harbinger Publications

**EATING MINDFULLY,
SECOND EDITION**

How to End Mindless Eating
& Enjoy a Balanced
Relationship with Food

ISBN 978-1608823307 / US $16.95

**THE UNBELIEVABLE
HAPPINESS OF WHAT IS**

Beyond Belief to Love,
Fulfillment &
Spiritual Awakening

ISBN 978-1626258716 / US $16.95

🌀 NON-DUALITY PRESS
An Imprint of New Harbinger Publications

new**harbinger**publications
1-800-748-6273 / newharbinger.com

(VISA, MC, AMEX / prices subject to change without notice)

Follow Us 📘 📧 📷 📌

Don't miss out on new books in the subjects that interest you.
Sign up for our Book Alerts at **newharbinger.com/bookalerts** 🖱

Register your **new harbinger** titles for additional benefits!

When you register your **new harbinger** title—purchased in any format, from any source—you get access to benefits like the following:

- Downloadable accessories like printable worksheets and extra content

- Instructional videos and audio files

- Information about updates, corrections, and new editions

Not every title has accessories, but we're adding new material all the time.

Access free accessories in 3 easy steps:

1. Sign in at NewHarbinger.com (or **register** to create an account).

2. Click on **register a book**. Search for your title and click the **register** button when it appears.

3. Click on the **book cover or title** to go to its details page. Click on **accessories** to view and access files.

That's all there is to it!

If you need help, visit:

NewHarbinger.com/accessories

new harbinger
CELEBRATING
40 YEARS